An Author's Guide
to Scholarly Publishing
and the Law

John C. Hogan
The RAND Corporation

Saul Cohen
Member of the California Bar

Prentice-Hall, Inc., Englewood Cliffs, N. J.

Library of Congress Catalog Card No.: 65-15563

Printed in the United States of America   C-05429

PRENTICE-HALL INTERNATIONAL, INC., *London*
PRENTICE-HALL OF AUSTRALIA, PTY., LTD., *Sydney*
PRENTICE-HALL OF CANADA, LTD., *Toronto*
PRENTICE-HALL OF INDIA (PRIVATE) LTD., *New Delhi*
PRENTICE-HALL OF JAPAN, INC., *Tokyo*

Preface

This is a book for the scholar and not for the lawyer (although hopefully the two are not mutually exclusive). Technical legal material, such as case citations, has been kept to a minimum. There are no footnotes. It is not the sort of book intended to make every man his own lawyer. There is a wise saying to the effect that a man who is his own lawyer has a fool for a client. With respect to many of the rules of law stated in the book, there are subtleties, qualifications, and exceptions which are omitted. If a scholar has a specific copyright problem that is not resolved by the information given in this book, he may wish to consult the works cited in the list of suggested readings. The wisest course, however, would be to consult a lawyer who is well versed in the copyright field. The local bar association or faculty members at a law school can probably recommend competent counsel if the scholar does not know a copyright lawyer. Although rules in every area of the law present uncertainties and ambiguities, this is particularly true of the law relating to the protection of literary, musical, and artistic works, for this is an area which is still developing, in which there are many unanswered questions, and in which the development has not always been consistent.

The book does not cover all of the scholar's legal problems. Each of us stands at the junction of a network of legal relations, and the law is with us always. Scholars have legal problems as homeowners, customers, employees, husbands, automobile drivers, and spectators at baseball games. The problems which this book surveys are those arising out of the scholar's activities as a scholar in connection with research and publication. It is not a handbook for administrators, although the authors believe much of the material will be of interest and use to administrators who deal with scholarly activities.

For the purposes of this book, the word "scholar" includes not only the university professor, but also everyone who is concerned with research, the publication of the results of that research, and the use of such published results—university professors, graduate students, foundation fellows, researchers in industry, doctoral candidates, scientists, engineers, journalists, and librarians.

In addition to the discussion of strictly legal problems, the book considers nonlegal matters relating to publication. It is through publication that the scholar reaches his public, which may be the vast lay audience or a small group of colleagues in his field. Publication is not only communication (an essential for the scientific community) but it is also the road to relative fame, if not fortune. A scholar's reputation is most often based upon his published work, and the reputation will survive dismal ineptness as a teacher. The slogan "publish or perish" is too well known in the university community to require comment.

Beginning with the term paper in his undergraduate years, the scholar progresses through the master's thesis and doctoral dissertation, technical articles in learned journals, contributions to a symposium volume, perhaps a lucky sale to the *Atlantic*, *Saturday Review*, or *Scientific American*, and then his first book. Publication is not only the primary means of establishing a reputation, it is often crucial to advancement.

After consideration of university publication requirements, we take a look, in Chapter 2, at various matters relating to journal publication by the scholar, including sources of income through magazine publication and the use of literary agents. The scholar's rights with respect to work that has not yet been published are considered in Chapter 3. Chapter 4 discusses publication in general and analyzes the terms of an ordinary book-publication contract. Chapters 5 and 6 discuss statutory copyright and the protection of published literary, artistic, and musical works. The book then turns, in Chapter 7, to a discussion of the legal problems involved in the scholar's use of the work of others, and considers, in Chapter 8, some particular categories of works of special interest to the scholar. Chapter 9 explains how to determine if a work is copyrighted, and Chapter 10 deals with problems arising out of the photoduplication of copyrighted material. Chapter 11 discusses materials which are not capable of copyright protection. The protection of inventions by patent is the subject of Chapter 12. Chapter 13 treats academic freedom and tenure. Some particular legal problems not relating to copyright, but perhaps of special interest to the scholar, are briefly discussed in Chapter 14.

Attached as appendices are the United States Copyright Law, Regulations of the Copyright Office, a sample copyright registration form, a list of adherents to the Universal Copyright Convention, a list of signatories to the Association of American University Presses Resolution on Permissions, a typical book-publication contract, a contract for a magazine article, and a list of suggested readings.

This book does not discuss the scholar's tax problems. Although there are certain tax questions of particular concern to the scholar (for example, whether a foundation grant is included in taxable income or whether the cost of books is deductable), changes in the tax laws and regulations may rapidly render specific comments obsolete. The scholar who wishes information on tax matters should consult one of the up-to-date tax guides, such as *Federal Tax Handbook,* published by Prentice-Hall and revised annually, and *Your Federal Income Tax,* published by the Internal Revenue Service and available from the local District Director of Internal Revenue or the Superintendent of Documents, Washington, D.C. 20402.

The idea for this book was conceived by John C. Hogan, whose suggestion met with enthusiasm on the part of the publisher. Mr. Hogan is primarily responsible for the materials in Chapters 1, 2, 4, and 12; Mr. Cohen for Chapters 3, 5 to 11, 13, and 14.

Those who read the manuscript and contributed to it by their comments and suggestions were: Mr. J. S. King, Jr., Treasurer, The RAND Corporation; Miss Dorothy Stewart, Chief Editor, The RAND Corporation; Mr. Paul Love, Reports Department, The RAND Corporation; and Mr. Stuart Cooney, The Systems Development Corporation. Many valuable comments on Chapter 12, "Patentable Inventions," were provided by Mr. Warren L. Patton of Fulwider, Patton, Rieber, Lee, and Utecht. Professor Morris Forkosch of Brooklyn Law School and Professor Mortimer Schwartz of the College of Law, University of Oklahoma, also read chapters of the manuscript and made constructive suggestions for improvements in the book. The manuscript was typed for book publication by Miss Pearl L. Leonhardt of The RAND Corporation.

J.C.H.

S.C.

Table of Contents

1

Scholarship and the universities

1. Doctoral Dissertations and Masters' Theses

The candidate for the Doctor of Philosophy Degree in letters, arts, and sciences is almost universally required to submit to his university, in partial fulfillment of the requirements for the degree, a written dissertation or thesis which is a contribution to knowledge in his field of study, which demonstrates his abilities for individual and original work, and which is expressed in satisfactory literary form. The *Examination Statutes* (1963) at Oxford University require that the work done by the student result in "an original contribution to knowledge deserving publication." Publication of the dissertation is expected and is encouraged. Formerly, the doctoral "thesis" was a collection of scholarly propositions that the candidate publicly defended with oral arguments before the faculty that was to confer the degree. Since the end of the nineteenth century, however, the word has signified a written work which the candidate prepares in partial satisfaction of the requirements for the degree.

The doctoral dissertation was once privately printed at the candidate's own expense and was distributed by him in a limited edition. A few of the older universities, especially in Europe, required that dissertations be printed and published before the degree was conferred; most universities now only require that the dissertation be in publishable form when it is presented to the committee. It is generally typewritten, the original copy being permanently deposited in the library of the university granting the degree. Obviously, not all dissertations will meet publishers' commercial book requirements, and the high cost of printing makes it impractical for universities to insist that scholars privately print and distribute their dissertations.

The standard set by the universities for the M.A. (*Magister Artium*) is considerably lower than that for the Ph.D. (*Philosophiae Doctor*). The master's thesis need not be an original contribution to knowledge, nor is it required to be published, although it should be in a form suitable for reproduction on microfilm. Candidates for this degree are encouraged by the universities to seek publication of parts of their theses in scholarly journals after the degree has been conferred.

Many worthy doctoral and masters' studies each year go wanting for a publisher. Recognizing this, the universities have adopted a scholarly and inexpensive method for making dissertations more widely available, namely, microfilming the typewritten manuscript and later, if desired, printing by Xerography through University Microfilms, Inc. of Ann Arbor, Michigan. This new development in graduate education raises interesting questions of copyright and patent law as these subjects apply to doctoral dissertations and masters' theses which are microfilmed.

2. University Policies on Publication

Because university requirements about publication of dissertations and theses, and abstracts thereof, are not all the same, the scholar should consult the catalog of his own institution for specific rules and policies. In general, however, the doctoral candidate has an option regarding the form in which his written work is acceptable—print or microfilm. For example:

> If the dissertation is accepted, the candidate must have it printed, lithoprinted, or microfilmed, according to a prescribed form. . . .

Copyright registration in the name of the University must be secured through the Manager of the University Press. Two hundred copies of the dissertation must be deposited in the Library of the University before the degree will be conferred.

Many universities require that typewritten dissertations be microfilmed at the candidate's expense, and signed contracts for this purpose are a condition precedent to conferring the degree. Such universities reserve the right to publish a printed abstract of the dissertation, in which case the abstract and a full typewritten copy of the dissertation suitable for microfilming must be submitted to the university.

Although printed publication of the dissertation is not generally a condition for conferring the doctorate, most universities expect it to occur within a "reasonably short time" after receipt of the degree. At the earliest practicable date after receipt of the degree, the candidate is encouraged to arrange for publication either of the whole dissertation or portions of it, and copies of the printed work must be deposited with the university. The candidate at one university is required to deposit a sum of money with the university guaranteeing printed publication of his dissertation, and failure to so publish within four years results in forfeiture of the deposit to the university.

Universities that make microfilming of the dissertation compulsory allow the candidate to take out the copyright in his own name. Doctoral dissertations that are published on microfilm through University Microfilms of Ann Arbor, Michigan, may be copyrighted by their authors. (See Chapter 6.) The original typewritten copy of the dissertation is used for microfilming, and the resulting microfilm copies are available for purchase by all who request them. Some university libraries have a collection of dissertations and theses which have been reproduced on microfilm.

A printed abstract of the dissertation is usually issued separately and also published in *Dissertation Abstracts*. Publication of the abstract does not prevent subsequent publication of a journal article based on the dissertation, and microfilming does not deprive the scholar of the right to subsequently publish his dissertation in book form.

Some universities expressly prohibit publication of any part of the dissertation before it is submitted to the committee without prior approval from the university. For example:

> If the student wishes to present as a thesis a published article, book, or other document, or a manuscript which has been accepted for publication, he must have the approval of his Division, Department, or Committee. In no case, however, may a thesis be presented which has already been presented in connection with candidacy for a degree either at this University or elsewhere.

Other universities have a rule on the prepublication of parts of theses and on joint authorship:

> With the approval of the department concerned, a portion of the thesis may consist of one or more articles published jointly by the candidate and members of the college staff or others. In any case, however, a substantial portion of the thesis must be the candidate's own exposition of his work.

At one college, in addition to the thesis, the candidate must also prepare a paper for publication embodying the results of his thesis work in whole or in part. This paper must either be accepted for publication or be in such form that the examining committee can expect it to be published. Joint authorship, except as noted above, is not permitted, but collaborative research by two or more graduate students is sometimes allowed for the masters' degree; there must, however, be enough independent effort to enable each candidate to make a separate contribution and to prepare an individual thesis.

Not all universities require a formal written thesis for the M.A. degree. This degree is sometimes granted as an incidental degree after completion of a portion of the requirements for the Ph.D. degree. Some departments require candidates for the M.A. to submit an "essay" in satisfaction of the written work for the degree, but other departments require no written work at all.

3. University Rights in Dissertations

Copyright in the dissertation, including the rights of publication, quotation, and so forth, do not always belong to the scholar after the dissertation has been accepted by the university. At one institution, dissertations are copyrighted in the name of the university and it is not "permitted for the author of the dissertation, either on his own account or through the agency of another person, to republish the dissertation in whole or in part until he has first arranged for the transfer of the copyright from the University to himself." Some universities expressly reserve literary rights in dissertations to the institution. Thus:

> Accepted theses or dissertations, with accompanying drawings, become the property of the University and are deposited in the University Library, where the duplicate copies are bound and made available for circulation. Permission to publish or adopt material in them must be secured from the appropriate Dean.

The scholar normally presents the original typewritten copy of the dissertation and the first carbon copy to the university; these are "the property of the University, and may not be published in whole or in part without written consent and due acknowledgment to the University." In general, however, the universities are silent on the matter of their rights in the dissertation, and where microfilming is compulsory, the candidate may copyright the dissertation in his own name.

Many scholars are working part-time in industry or on government contracts while studying for an advanced degree at a university. Their research for industry and their work at the university for the degree frequently is the same, especially in the fields of science and engineering, and also in some social sciences. The employer may require written reports periodically on the scholar's findings, and these reports are published by the company, either with or without copyright. The employment contract invariably contains a clause assigning to the company legal rights to all writings in the performance of the scholar's work for the company, and this includes written materials that may subsequently be included in the dissertation. Furthermore, if the research and the writing is done under a government contract, the United States government has a royalty-free nonexclusive license to use and to reproduce the report anywhere in the world for any governmental purpose. Publication of the company report cannot generally be delayed until after the dissertation has been submitted to the university and the degree is conferred, yet if chapters from the dissertation are previously published as company reports the dissertation may be unacceptable to the doctoral committee and the scholar may not receive the degree.

Where the employment contract conveys ownership to the company and the right to publish written materials, the scholar must seek agreement with the university before company publication of material that will also be used in the dissertation.

4. Acceptability of the Dissertation

The acceptability of the dissertation for the degree is dependent upon approval of the final manuscript by a faculty committee appointed for that purpose, approval being evidenced by their signature on a special form. Some universities require that such approval be unanimous; others require that only a majority of the committee sign. The basis for approval of the dissertation is generally stated in broad terms. For example:

> The dissertation must give evidence of the candidate's ability to carry on independent investigation and must be satisfactory in style and composition. It must represent a definite contribution to the knowledge of his subject, must be the result of independent work, must include original research, and must in some way add to or otherwise modify what was previously known on the subject.

Although it is convenient to define requirements for the Doctor of Philosophy degree in terms of credits and examinations, universities are careful to point out that no number of credits or routine compliance with regulations entitles a student to this degree. It is conferred solely in recognition of high attainments in the chosen field of scholarship, and the universities reserve to themselves the decision as to the excellence of the student's work and his satisfactory performance of the requirements for the degree.

In the case of the doctoral dissertation, the committee is the sole judge of satisfactory performance. A committeeman who refuses to agree to confer the degree because of dissatisfaction with the dissertation probably could not be compelled to do so by a court of law; if his refusal is for "other reasons," a court might issue a writ compelling consent on a proper showing of facts.

A few law cases involving the right of a student to receive an academic degree have been decided, and in most of these, the courts have refused to interfere with the exercise of discretion by the proper university authorities. Where a doctoral dissertation was rejected by the committee and the candidate subsequently sued the university, the court admitted that a proper case of this nature might be maintained against a private university, but said that it was within the discretion of the university's authorities to reject the candidate's dissertation because there was ample evidence to support the refusal of the dissertation and because it had not been established that the rejection "was arbitrary, capricious, or unreasonable." The courts will not substitute their own opinion as to the merits of a doctoral dissertation for that of the faculty members whom the university has selected to make such a determination.

Although the courts will not review the discretion of the university faculty in refusing to permit a student to receive a degree, yet if there is an absolute and arbitrary refusal, there is no exercise of discretion—it is nothing but a wilful violation of the duties which the faculty have assumed. The proper procedure to be followed by university disciplinary committees has been described as follows:

> It is not necessary that the professors should go through the formality of a trial. They should give the student whose conduct is being investigated every fair opportunity of showing his innocence. They should be careful in receiving evidence against him. They should weigh it; determine whether it comes from a source freighted with prejudice; determine the likelihood, by all surrounding circumstances, as to who is right, and then act upon it as jurors with calmness, consideration, and fair minds. When they have done this and reached a conclusion, they have done all that the law requires them to do.

5. Title of the Dissertation

The scholar is usually required to file the title of his dissertation with the university. He is allowed to choose any title he wishes, provided that it is descriptive of the contents of the dissertation. He may even adopt a title previously used by another scholar on a published book. Titles to dissertations, books, or scholarly articles cannot be copyrighted. Works are registered at the Copyright Office under their titles for the purpose of identification, and no protection is thereby afforded to the title. (See Chapter 11, Section 2.)

6. "Publish or Perish"

Even in classical times educated men were concerned about publication of their writings. "I am myself a good deal backwards in publishing," wrote Pliny to his friend Suetonius Tranquillas, "but your slowness and hesitancy are more than a match for even mine." Thoughtful men of all ages have exhorted scholars to publish, while others have queried the reasonableness of the writing requirement. When his sonnet was rejected, Charles Lamb exclaimed: "Damn the age; I will write for Antiquity!"

Publication is the surest way to professional recognition in most fields. Large universities and prestige colleges generally require it of their faculty members. Although this requirement is not always formally spelled out in university regulations, the conditions for advancement in rank and salary, acquiring tenure, grants for research and travel, reduced teaching loads, and similar forms of special treatment for professors who publish show that publication is encouraged and expected of faculty members. One of the four "Criteria for Appointment and Promotion" at a large university is:

> *Research and Creative Work*—Evidence of a productive and creative mind should be sought in the candidate's published research or recognized artistic production in original architectural or engineering designs, or the like.
>
> Publications in research and other creative accomplishment should be evaluated, not merely enumerated. There should be evidence that the candidate is continuously and effectively engaged in creative activity of high quality and significance. Work in progress should be assessed wherever possible. Account should be taken of the type and quality of creative activity normally expected in the candidate's field. Appraisals of publications or other works in the scholarly and critical literature provide important testimony.
>
> Textbooks, reports, circulars, and similar publications normally considered evidence of teaching ability or public service, or contribu-

tions by candidates in the professional school faculties to the professional literature or the advancement of professional practice or of professional education, should be judged creative work only if they present new ideas or incorporate scholarly research.

In certain fields, such as art, architecture, music, literature, and drama, distinguished creation should receive consideration equivalent to that distinction attained in research. In evaluating artistic creativity, an attempt should be made to define the candidate's merit in the light of such criteria as originality, scope, richness, and depth of creative expression.

Universities frequently maintain a "Faculty Research Fund," out of which special grants are made for research travel, research supplies, research equipment, research assistance, and the purchase of reprints. Where the editing of scholarly journals is a recognized activity of faculty members, the teaching load of those who serve as editors of such journals is sometimes reduced.

The requirement to publish is not limited to university men, but also exists in research organizations. Here the scholar or scientist is generally hired exclusively to do research and to write, there being no students to teach; even the scientist who spends his life mostly in the laboratory must eventually write reports and publish his findings if the rest of the world is to know of his discoveries or inventions. What, therefore, are the purposes and aims of scholarly authorship, and what does it accomplish?

7. The Purposes of Scholarly Authorship

Six centuries ago, a gifted researcher and experienced writer who authored a monumental history of the world set down in writing what he conceived as the prime purpose of scholarly composition. The man was Ibn Khaldûn (1332-1406), a professor, judge, politician, and college president. His seven-volume book, written in Arabic, has been translated today by Franz Rosenthal as *The Muqaddimah: An Introduction to History*, 3 Vols. (New York: Pantheon Books, Inc., 1958). The purposes of scholarly authorship, as Ibn Khaldûn saw them, might be classified under seven headings:

Creation

The "invention of a science with its subject, its division into chapters and sections, and the discussion of its problems." Not every scholar however, can conceive of the first principles of a new science, and so there exists the lesser task of "invention of problems and topics of research" that one wishes to communicate to others.

Interpretation

The discussion and works of earlier writers may be difficult to understand, but one who possesses a knowledge and understanding of them himself may want "to communicate his knowledge to someone else who may perhaps have difficulties with the same problems, so that all who are worthy may have the benefit of his knowledge."

Correction

If one finds an error or mistake in the work of an earlier scholar, and if he has proof of it, he may want "to communicate this discovery to those after him, since it is impossible to eradicate a mistake in the work in question in view of its wide dissemination in space and time, the fame of the author, and the reliance people place on his learning." The correction is published so subsequent scholars may benefit by knowledge of it.

Completion

A "particular discipline may be incomplete, certain problems or details requiring treatment." Scholarly authorship completes or perfects such a discipline by providing the lacking problems and by adequate treatment of the details of the discipline so that the incompleteness no longer exists.

Arrangement

The "problems of a particular science may have been treated without proper arrangement into chapters and without order." This circumstance affords an opportunity to arrange and improve on the problems of the discipline, placing each in the proper chapter where it belongs.

Collection

The "problems of a certain science might only exist scattered among the proper chapters of other sciences." A scholar may recognize this and undertake to collect the problems from among the other disciplines, in which case "a new discipline will make its appearance."

Abridgment

Something "in the main scholarly work may be too long and prolix," in which case "to compose a brief and succinct abridgment, omitting all repetitions, is possible."

Two examples of ignorance and impudence, Ibn Khaldûn said, have no place in scholarly authorship. One is the practice whereby a dishonest person attempts "to ascribe the work of an earlier author to himself with the aid of certain tricks, such as changing the wording and the arrangement of the contents" of a book and republishing it under his own name. The other is one in which a person might "eliminate material essential to a particular discipline, or mention unnecessary material, or replace correct statements with wrong ones, or mention useless material."

8. Controversies Between Scholars

The academic world attaches extraordinary value to a man's reputation for honesty and for fair dealing, yet sometimes a dispute arises over the authorship of an article that discusses a new theory or method. The natural reluctance of scholars to settle such controversies by law—and, in fact, there may be no legal cause of action—has caused some professional groups to adopt their own procedures for collecting the facts and deciding if there has been a misuse by one scholar of another's unpublished materials.

When two scholars, both claiming priority, have written up a theory for journal publication, the professional society may appoint a third party, generally a senior professor in the field, to act as judge in the matter. This professor will request from each of the disputing authors a carefully written statement of their relationship to each other in the research that gave rise to the dispute. If the material has not yet appeared in print, the editor of the journal having it under consideration may withhold publication until the dispute has been resolved.

A controversy of this nature almost always injures the reputation of both parties, even the one that is blameless. The sole interest of the society in the matter is to terminate the controversy justly, and, if possible, quickly. The only action that the society might take against the offending member is a disciplinary one, perhaps expulsion.

The author of a published book is regarded in law as having invited public judgment of his book, and he cannot complain to the courts of anyone's adverse opinions, comments, or criticisms of the book. No legal action can be taken against a reviewer if his words are fair and bona fide comments upon the contents of the book. (See Chapter 15, Section 1.) Some journals, however, will permit the author of the book to reply to his reviewer if the review is adverse and especially if it contains misstatements of fact. The author's reply is generally sent to the reviewer so that he may also respond to it. However, an author's request to see the reviewer's reply prior to publication is usually denied.

The preparation of multiple translations of foreign-language works, especially Russian books, has led to controversies between scholars over which scholar has the right to publish his translation. This frequently becomes a controversy involving publishers too, especially if two or more publishing houses have contracted for the different translations. It is generally agreed among the publishers that the first publishing house to announce the translation in *Pub-*

lishers' Weekly, the journal of the trade, has priority right to publish the book. In order to avoid duplication of effort among scholars in preparing and publishing translations, the U.S. Department of Commerce (Office of Technical Services, Washington, D.C. 20230) provides a reference service for the location and identification of translated materials, both completed translations and translations in process. *Technical Translations,* a bimonthly publication of the Office of Technical Services, contains an up-to-date list of "Translations in Process."

2

The scholar writes

1. Contributions to Scholarly Journals

Most writings of the scholar will be either books or contributions
to periodicals. (Books are discussed in Chapter 4.) Contributions
by scholars to periodicals are generally articles published in the professional journals that specialize in the scholar's field and for which
there is no monetary compensation. The scholar that publishes an
article in such a journal may later want to reprint the same material, with minor changes, as a chapter in a book he is writing or
to make other use of it.

The question of who holds the copyright in the article, the author
or the journal, arises at the time the manuscript is submitted to a
book publisher. The book contract will require the scholar to convey to the publisher both domestic and foreign publication rights to
the manuscript. If the article was copyrighted in the name of the
journal, the scholar will be unable to comply with this without first
obtaining the consent of the journal.

Some professional journals are not copyrighted, and the articles
they publish are in the public domain, unless the scholar expressly
requests copyright and the journal consents to print the appropriate
notice on the article. Most professional journals are copyrighted,

however, and the articles they publish are protected—but the copyright is in the name of the journal, not in the author's name. (See Chapter 8, Section 10.) Therefore the scholar should, at the time of publication, arrange with the editor of the journal for retention of the right to make further use of the article, either as a chapter in his proposed book or as classroom study material. There is a reluctance among some journals to print separate copyright notices, and a natural embarrassment among scholars to request copyright in their own names.

Some professional journals have a policy against acceptance of manuscripts that have been copyrighted, previously published, or submitted for publication elsewhere. Other journals ask authors for a complete release of rights in the manuscripts they publish. Examples are:

> *Operations Research.* Submission of a manuscript to the editor is representation that it has been neither copyrighted nor published, that it is not being submitted for publication elsewhere, and that, if the work results from a military contract, it has been released for open publication.
>
> *Journal of the Society for Industrial and Applied Mathematics.* When manuscripts are submitted for publication, such action is representation by the author that the manuscript has not been copyrighted, published, or submitted for publication elsewhere.
>
> *Archive for Rational Mechanics and Analysis.* For all articles published, exclusive rights in all languages and countries rest with the publisher. Without express permission of the publisher, no reproduction of any kind is allowed.
>
> *The Journal of Physiology.* Papers submitted for publication must be accompanied by the following declaration: "The attached paper entitled . . . has not been, and is not intended to be published elsewhere except in the *Journal of Physiology,* and we/I agree that, if and when it is accepted by the Editors for publication, in consideration for such acceptance the entire copyright in this paper shall pass thereupon to the Physiological Society." The Society normally honors requests from authors to reproduce their own papers, but permission is not given to third parties except with the consent of the authors concerned.
>
> *Journal of Mathematics and Mechanics.* The submission of a paper implies assurance on the part of the author that the paper has not been "widely circulated" by the organization with which he is associated, nor has it been copyrighted, published, or submitted for publication elsewhere.

Some scholarly journals have established page publication charges which are paid by the author or the firm for which he works. The purpose of such charges is to help defray costs of printing and publishing the journals, for many journals do not accept advertising and the subscription rates are not adequate to cover these costs; one journal states, moreover, that an author may avoid delay in publication by paying the costs of publishing his own article. Page charges are usually calculated as part of the cost of composition and make-up of the journals. Federal research grants and contracts may allow for such charges. Four criteria adopted by the government for honoring page charge bills submitted by journal publishers are:

(1) The research papers report on work supported by the government.

(2) The charges are levied impartially on all research papers published by the journals, whether by nongovernment or by government authors.

(3) Payment of such charges is in no sense a condition for acceptance of manuscripts by the journal.

(4) The journals involved are not operated for profit.

Some examples of journals that have page publication charges are:

The Physical Review. Authors' institutions are requested to pay a publication charge of $50.00 per page which, if honored, entitles them to one hundred free reprints. An additional $10.00 is requested for prepublication of the abstract in *Physics Abstracts*.

Duke Mathematical Journal. To cover part of the cost of publication, authors' institutions are billed a publication charge of $20.00 per page, and payment of this charge entitles the authors to one hundred free reprints.

The Journal of Psychology. The author receives two hundred free reprints of his article, but is charged the actual manufacturing costs of any zincs, halftone cuts, or expensive tables and equations. There is also a page publication charge ranging from $40.00 for a four-page signature to $400.00 for a forty-page signature. However, these "charges are tentative and will be adjusted as justified."

Psychological Review. Because of the large number of manuscripts submitted to this journal, there is a publication lag of several months. "Authors may avoid this delay if they are prepared to pay the costs of publishing their own articles; the appearance of articles by other contributors is not thereby delayed."

American Institute of Aeronautics and Astronautics Journal. Authors' institutions are requested to pay a publication charge of $40.00 per page, with a minimum of $40.00 per Note or Comment, which charge, if honored, entitles them to one hundred free reprints.

American Journal of Physics. Authors' institutions are requested to pay an optional publication charge of $25.00 per page—which, when honored, entitles them to one hundred free reprints—plus a $10.00 per article charge towards the support of its abstracting and indexing in *Physics Abstracts.*

Journal of Mathematics and Physics. The institution with which the author is associated is requested to pay a publication charge of $5.00 per page, in return for one hundred and fifty reprints of the article.

2. Contributions to Magazines That Pay

The scholar who writes articles for the popular journals and magazines expects to be paid, and such magazines generally acquire all rights in the articles they publish. If the product of scholarly research is suitable for publication in a learned journal as well as in a book and in a magazine that pays, the scholar should contract with the magazine publisher for the rights he wishes to retain in his materials. An article that is suitable for a professional sociology journal, for example, may be popularized for publication also in *The Saturday Evening Post,* and if the author retains the book publication rights, he can likewise include it in a textbook.

A list of magazines that pay for the materials they publish will be found in the *Writer's Market,* which gives some 3,500 American markets for freelance writers, and in *The Writers' and Artists' Year Book,* a British directory for writers and artists. Both sources contain information about the kinds of materials wanted by the magazines and the rates paid.

The sale of an article to a magazine usually involves a legal assignment of rights in writing from the author to the publisher. The assignment may include the following matters, and any others that the parties are inclined to include in it:

Grant of rights

All rights of every kind in the material, including the right to copyright it in the publisher's name, may be transferred to the publisher by the assignment. Some publishers also acquire the right not only to use the author's name in connection with the published article, but also his biography and likeness (either a photograph or a sketch) to advertise the issue of the magazine in which the article appears. It is possible to negotiate with the publisher for book publication and other rights in the article and for the author to retain these by expressly saying so in the assignment.

Copyright

The magazine normally acquires the right to copyright the article in its own name, and the author agrees to execute all documents required to secure such copyright in the first instance and to execute all documents necessary to renew the copyright; he also agrees to sign necessary papers to protect the copyright in case of an infringement.

Author's rights

The publisher may purchase first serial publication rights only, or he may acquire all magazine and book rights to the material, including reprint rights. Some assignments provide that after one complete publication of the material in the magazine, the publisher will reassign to the author on written request all rights except magazine rights. The author can thus secure for himself the book publication rights in his material by reassignment, if the original document contains such a provision.

Motion-picture and television rights

Motion-picture and television rights in the material can be reserved exclusively to the author, or they may be handled under some joint sharing arrangement with respect to the ownership of such rights and the royalties received from the sale thereof.

Author's responsibilities

The author generally agrees to protect the publisher's copyright by affixing a proper copyright notice in connection with any future publication made by him of the material as permitted under the assignment. When selling or transferring rights reserved to the author, he agrees to give written notice to the buyer of such rights of the terms of the original assignment.

First serial or magazine publication right refers to the right to publish all or part of the material in a magazine or newspaper either before it is published as a book or later in condensation. Such rights can be withheld by the scholar when signing the book-publication contract if the manuscript appears to be suitable for magazine or newspaper serialization. The market for first serial publication includes such magazines as *The Saturday Evening Post, Look, Life, Harpers', Atlantic,* and other magazines which publish condensed versions of books in installments, condense a book in a single installment, or publish chapters from books. Newspapers sometimes buy the right to serialize a book by publishing it in installments.

3. Literary Agents

It is not necessary to retain a literary agent to locate a publisher for a scholarly book or to place an article with a scientific or learned journal. Because such journals normally do not pay fees for the materials they publish, agents do not operate in their fields. Publishers' representatives (See Chapter 4) will help the scholar arrange for publication of his scholarly book-length manuscript.

This is not to say, however, that the scholar never needs an agent; on the contrary, an agent can be of great value when negotiating with magazines that pay for material or in placing a novel, play, television or motion-picture script with a publisher or producer. In the first place, the scholar who writes a trade book (See Chapter 4, Section 4) will probably have had no experience in negotiating contract rights to such a book, especially the important subsidiary rights. A good agent can secure a better financial arrangement than the scholar could secure alone.

The role of the agent includes the location of suitable paying publisher outlets for his client's writings and the handling of contract and business arrangements when there is a sale; he may even suggest subjects for which there is a market. If the agent makes a bad financial arrangement for publication of his client's book, both suffer by loss of potential income and the agent by the ultimate loss of his client.

Writers whose materials sell are sought after by agents, but young and unknown writers are apt to have difficulty. Not all agents will accept unsolicited manuscripts. Some require proof of previous sales to publishers before they will consider the work of a new writer. Most agents, however, do accept some new talent, even without previous sales, if they believe the writer has promise. Sometimes unknown authors must pay a reading fee.

In the case of motion pictures and television, it is usually necessary and probably wise to have an agent, because the studios and the producers refuse to read unsolicited scripts submitted by individuals. Some agents specialize in these fields, just as others specialize in the book or magazine fields.

The scholar who wants a literary agent will find a list in the *Writer's Market* and in *The Literary Market Place*. The scholar simply writes a letter to the agent, asking if he will accept him as a client.

4. Compensation of Authors

The basis for compensating authors varies from field to field; some authors are paid a royalty on their work and others an outright fee or salary. The practices in the principal artistic fields are summarized on the following pages.

Book publishers

The author of a book usually receives a royalty computed either as a percentage of the list (retail) price of the book or as a percentage of the publisher's net receipts from the sale of the book. (See also Chapter 4, Section 2.) During recent years, the average royalty payment to book authors has been between 10 and 11 per cent of the publishers' net receipts.

Magazine publishers

Magazine publishers purchase literary materials for at least first serial publication rights, and they pay either a flat fee or so much per word for the articles they publish. Some magazines use photographs, and they pay for these in addition to the payment for the article.

Music publishers

Music publishers generally hold the copyrights to musical materials in accordance with the contracts they have with the composer-lyricists. It is not uncommon for not less than 50 per cent of royalties received by the music publisher to be paid to the composer-lyricist.

Reference book publishers

The publishers of reference works, such as the *Encyclopaedia Britannica*, pay so much per word for the articles of their contributor. Writing for reference books is by invitation of the publisher only. The publisher's staff frequently create articles in their own right as editors and compilers of the books.

Newspaper publishers make direct salary payments to their editorial staffs, columnists, cartoonists, and feature writers. They sometimes purchase free-lance copyrightable materials, and they may buy the serialization rights to books.

Advertising

The advertising industry is involved in the preparation and placing of written and artistic matter in the various advertising media—newspapers, magazines, television, and radio. Payments are made either on a salary or free-lance basis for creative, artistic, and literary talent employed by the advertising agencies to produce the needed advertising materials.

Radio, television, and motion pictures

The principal groups receiving payments for the use of their creative works on radio and television are the writers of story materials and the composer-lyricists. Story writers are paid, either on a free-lance contractual basis or on an employment basis, for original scripts or for the adaptation of published literary material for broadcast use. The Writers Guild of America has established for its members certain minimum rates to be paid to television writers for the "narrative synopsis," the "story," the "teleplay," and the "story and teleplay." There are also minimum rates for rewriting or polishing a script. Royalties paid the television writer for broadcasts of his material are known as "residuals." Residual payments for the use of literary materials on television can sometimes be substantial.

Motion-picture producers employ creative talent for the writing and adaptation of story materials for the screen, usually on an employment-for-hire basis. The producers also purchase motion-picture rights to novels, stories, or other material from the publishers or others who hold the copyrights. Usually, a large portion of the purchase price of the motion-picture rights to a novel goes to the author of the book, and book publishers generally retain only a 10 per cent fee. It has been estimated that 5 per cent of the average production budget of the motion-picture industry is paid for story costs, that is, payments made to writers and adaptors of story materials and to owners of the copyrights.

5. Using Classified Information

Information which requires protection in the interest of national defense is known as "classified information." There are three categories of such information: *Confidential*, *Secret*, and *Top Secret*. In addition, there is a marking known as *Restricted Data*.

Defense information and material which, if compromised, could *prejudice or injure* the defense of the nation is classified as *Confidential*. Defense information and material, the unauthorized disclosure of which could result in *serious* damage to the United States, is classified *Secret*. Information and material, the defense aspect of which is paramount and the unauthorized disclosure of which could result in exceptionally *grave* damage to the United States, is classified *Top Secret*. Information concerning the design, manufacture, and production of nuclear weapons or materials is classified as *Restricted Data*.

Access to classified information is a privilege, not a right. Scholars working in industry may have been granted security clearances which limit their level of access to classified information. The care and handling of classified information are subjects discussed with the security officer at the time the scholar receives his clearance. In general, classified information can not be shown to, or discussed with, other persons who do not have the proper security clearance and the "need to know." When classified information is disclosed orally, it must be clearly identified as such to the hearers.

Material assigned any of the security classifications listed above cannot be published in a book or in any of the scholarly journals or popular magazines. This would constitute a security violation, and the scholar would be liable to prosecution under federal laws.

There have been cases where classified information was created, even though the research was based entirely upon unclassified source materials. Accordingly, if the scholar does not have a security clearance, and if he has written something which deals with military applications, government operations, or national policy which he thinks should be submitted for security review, he should send his material as a private citizen to the Directorate of Security Review, Office of the Assistant Secretary (Public Affairs), Department of Defense, Washington, D.C. 20301. He will be notified in writing by the government that the material is unclassified, or if the material is classified, he will be provided with guidance on how it should be handled.

3

Rights in unpublished works

1. Common Law Copyright

The scholar has completed his article on the use of prepositions
in old French or the influence of the insurance business on Wallace
Stevens' poetry. He has heard that his work should be "copyrighted"
to prevent its unauthorized use by others. He may also have heard
that he should send himself a copy by registered mail or send something to Washington. It is commonly thought that *something* must
be done to copyright a literary work. This is one of many prevalent
misconceptions about copyright.

Upon the creation of any literary, artistic, or musical work,
whether it be a poem, painting, short story, song, or scholarly mono-
graph, the work is automatically protected against copying or
"plagiarism" by what is frequently referred to as the "common law
copyright." The creator has the right to determine when, where, and
by whom his work shall first be made public. The common law
copyright is sometimes called the "right of first publication." In
many states there are statutes codifying the common law protection.
Unlike federal copyright protection, which is limited to a maximum
of fifty-six years, this protection for unpublished literary, musical,
and artistic works is perpetual. It is precisely this perpetual nature
of common law protection that sometimes creates difficulties for

the scholar who wishes to quote from or reprint unpublished letters, diaries, and other manuscripts.

Note the word *unpublished*, for this is the key word in connection with common law protection. Once a work has been *published*, within the special meaning of that word as used in copyright law, compliance with the federal copyright law is required or the work falls into the public domain and may be freely copied by anyone. What constitutes "publication" is discussed in Section 2 of this chapter. Remember then that with respect to an unpublished work, the copyright protection is automatic and no special notice need be placed on the work, nor need any other steps be taken.

Certain kinds of unpublished works may, but need not, be registered for copyright under the federal copyright law. See Section 4 of this chapter for a discussion of registration of unpublished works.

To understand the nature of copyright, it should be kept in mind that the copyright is an intangible right ("incorporeal," as lawyers sometimes say), and is distinct from the property right in the material object. As the Copyright Act puts it:

> The copyright is distinct from the property in the material object copyrighted, and the sale or conveyance, by gift or otherwise, of the material object shall not of itself constitute a transfer of the copyright, nor shall the assignment of the copyright constitute a transfer of the title to the material object. . . .

Obviously the purchase of a book in a bookstore does not give the purchaser any interest in the copyright, although he is free to sell the book or dog-ear its pages. The purchaser of a painting from an artist may not have the right to permit the making of reproductions of the painting, and the recipient of a letter does not have the right to common law copyright in the letter. (See Chapter 8, Section 1.)

A well known rare-book dealer purchased in 1945 the original handwritten and autographed manuscript of a Mark Twain short story. He asked permission of the owner of all the literary properties which had belonged to Mark Twain and had not been otherwise disposed of for permission to publish the work, but permission was refused. The book dealer went ahead with publication anyway and suit was brought to prevent him from publishing the story or reproducing it in any way. The highest court of New York state held that since there was no proof that Mark Twain had ever transferred his right of first publication, the book dealer had not acquired that right when he bought the manuscript.

2. Publication

The dividing line between the common law copyright and protection under the federal copyright statute is the act of publication. Up to the point of publication, protection is given by the common law (or applicable state statute) and continues forever. Thereafter the author must look to the federal law for protection, and that protection is given only for a specified number of years. If the line is crossed without complying with the requirements of the federal law, the work has no protection.

Unfortunately the word "publication" is not defined in the copyright statute. The question of the proper definition of publication is one that has exercised legal scholars, and the problem has not yet been resolved. New cases continue to be greeted with criticism or approval as they attempt to draw the invisible line. Common sense is of no help in this connection. Placing a book on sale in a bookstore may be a publication even though no one buys a copy for six months, whereas the performance of a hit Broadway play seen by thousands over a five-year period is not a publication. Generally speaking, the public sale or other unrestricted distribution of a work constitutes a publication. One legal authority has defined it this way:

> Publication occurs when by consent of the copyright owner, the original or tangible copies of a work are sold, leased, loaned, given away, or otherwise made available to the general public, or when an authorized offer is made to dispose of the work in any such manner even if a sale or other such disposition does not in fact occur. (See Nimmer, Appendix H.)

Each copy of the work, when published, must bear a proper copyright notice. If the work is published without a proper notice it becomes a part of the public domain and may be freely copied or reprinted by anyone. What constitutes a proper notice is fully discussed in Chapter 6, Section 1.

Communication of the substance of the work or the distribution of copies to others under restricted or limited circumstances is not a publication. The expression "limited publication" is used to describe the kind of distribution which does not constitute such a publication that it divests the work of its common law copyright protection. Submission of the work to friends or other scholars for review does not constitute a publication. Whether or not we call it a "limited" publication, it is clear that it does not constitute such publication as would put the work into the public domain if the notice requirements of the Copyright Act are not complied with. Issuing copies to students in a particular class for their use in connection with testing the quality of the work as a teaching tool is not a publication. Submission of a draft of a speech or proposed book chapter to members of a colloquium does not constitute a publication. Sale of copies in a campus book store, however, where they could be purchased by anyone, would constitute publication, as would the indiscriminate distribution of copies or wholesale distribution to friends and fellow scholars without restriction; unless it bears the proper copyright notice, the work would under such circumstances fall into the public domain. When the work is being distributed to a limited audience for a limited purpose, it is suggested that an appropriate legend be placed on the work, such as "For use in Seminar on Economic Development in the Amazon Basin only" or "Preliminary. Not for publication or quotation." If copies are distributed in a manner that does not constitute a publication, it does not matter whether they are returned or not. Of course, insistence upon their being returned might be a positive factor bearing upon whether the distribution is only a "limited" publication. Distribution to friends or colleagues should be accomplished by a letter or note along the following lines: "I am enclosing an article of mine which has not yet been published. I am circulating a few copies among friends and colleagues to whom I think it will be of interest for possible comment and criticism. It is intended for your personal use." There is no specific number of copies which can be safely distributed.

Although the cases speak of a publication without notice as an "abandonment of the copyright" or a "dedication to the public," the writer's intent is irrelevant. Whether he intends to do so or not, a publication without notice results in loss of the copyright forever.

It should be noted that the concept of publication does not have the significance in foreign copyright law that it does in American copyright law. It is only in the United States that there is a dual system of protection for literary and artistic work: the protection of unpublished works under state law and the protection of published works under the federal copyright statute.

3. Priority of Conception

Priority of conception is of no significance in copyright law, unlike the situation with respect to patent law. (See Chapter 12.) If a poet were to copyright his poem and by rare chance another poet were to later write a substantially identical poem without ever having seen the first poem, both poets could validly copyright their poems. (Of course, a suit for copyright infringement under such circumstances presents obvious problems of proof.) Copyright protects only against copying. Unlike patent law, it does not protect against independent conception.

If for some reason a scholar should wish to establish the date of the writing of a piece of work, the best method is to have one or more colleagues read it, initial each of the pages, and write a simple statement on the last page to the following effect: "At the request of Schuyler Scholar, I read the foregoing manuscript this March 17, 1964." This method is preferable to the old and not very useful device of mailing oneself a copy by registered mail.

Establishing the date on which the scholar commences work on a book may have tax relevance. (See Chapter 14.) Early research notes and the first draft should be dated. Affidavits from colleagues would be helpful.

4. Registration of Unpublished Works

Although the scholar must normally look to the common law copyright for protection of his unpublished work, certain kinds of unpublished works are eligible for federal statutory protection. Works which are not reproduced for sale and which are intended primarily for performance or exhibition, such as lectures, plays, television scripts, musical compositions, paintings, drawings, sculpture, photographs, and motion pictures, may be copyrighted under Section 12 of the Copyright Act. This requires sending the proper registration form (See Chapter 6, Section 2) and the prescribed fee of $4.00 to the Copyright Office. The application must be accompanied by one complete copy, if the work is a lecture, play, script, or musical composition. If the work is a painting, drawing, or sculpture, a photograph or other identifying reproduction must be submitted. If it is a motion picture, there must be submitted one print (that is, one frame or blowup) taken from each scene or act (if it is a photoplay) or at least two prints taken from different sections of the motion picture (if it is not a photoplay), together with the title and description of the film in the form of a synopsis or continuity. For the difference between "motion-picture photoplays" and "motion pictures other than photoplays," see Chapter 8, Section 9.

The twenty-eight-year original copyright term begins on the date of deposit of the application and copy in the Copyright Office, even though the work is later published. If the work is later published, the usual copyright registration procedure (outlined in Chapter 6, Section 2) should be followed, including the deposit of copies of the published work. If the work is later published, it must of course bear a proper copyright notice. The year date in the notice (where a date is required, that is, on literary, musical, and dramatic works) should be the year in which the copyright was secured under the provisions of the Copyright Act, that is, the year of the registration as an unpublished work, not the year of subsequent publication.

If the subsequently published work involves substantial new matter, then there is justification for claiming a new copyright and using the subsequent year. A safe approach under such circumstances would be to include both years in the notice. See Chapter 6, Section 5 for a discussion of new versions and new matter in an older work.

4

Publishing your book

1. How to Find a Publisher
for a Book

The scholar seeking a publisher for his book should begin by consulting the current edition of *The Literary Market Place* (New York: R. R. Bowker Company), a directory of the American book publishing trade which lists the names and addresses of over five hundred publishers in the United States and which gives their fields of publishing interest. *The Literary Market Place* also contains a wealth of useful information about book publishing in general, including lists of free-lance editorial and translation services, names and addresses of literary agents, publishers' representatives, book reviewers, columnists, clipping bureaus, literary prizes and awards, and lists of newspapers and magazines. If the scholar desires to publish his book abroad, the *Publishers' International Year Book* and *The Writers' and Artists' Year Book* provide information about publishers in Europe and England.

The next step in locating a publisher would be to survey the important books in the field of the manuscript to find out which publishers issued them. "A publisher that is active in a certain field of scholarship is likely to be interested in more manuscripts in that field," wrote Herbert S. Bailey, Jr., Director of the Princeton University Press, "and he is also likely to do a better job of publishing in that field." The advice of colleagues who have published with these houses—the ones that are active in the particular field of scholarship—is also helpful to the scholar. By examining the important books published in his field, the scholar may be able to identify some colleagues whose experience he can solicit.

It is not necessary to retain a literary agent to find a publisher for a scholarly book. (See Chapter 2, Section 3.) The larger commercial publishing houses have separate departments for scientific and technical books, college and high school textbooks, business books, law books, and so forth. Field representatives of these departments canvass industry and the college campuses seeking book-length manuscripts for publication. The author of a scholarly work, therefore, need only write to the main office of a publisher and make it known that he has a book-length manuscript available; in many cases the publisher's field representative will call on him personally to discuss the manuscript and its publication possibilities. Since university presses do not normally have field representatives, it is necessary to communicate with them by mail or telephone. A letter to the director of a university press will elicit a reply indicating whether the press is interested in the manuscript and whether it should be mailed to them for review and consideration.

In talking with publishers' representatives, the scholar should inquire about the following items, some of which will later be written into the publication contract: (1) The royalty schedule; (2) Approximate publication date; (3) The general format of the book; (4) The publisher's estimate of sales, generally for a three- to five-year period; (5) Promotional and advertising plans for the book; (6) The proposed price of the book.

The book should be priced competitively with other works on the same subject. It is also important to ask if the book will be included in a series, and how it will be advertised and promoted in connection with other successful books on the publisher's list. In the case of a college textbook, it is well to inquire about the publisher's sales staff for reaching the university and college market. (See Section 4 of this chapter.)

A publisher cannot generally be held accountable for a lost manuscript if it is sent to him unsolicited, but if the scholar writes to the publisher and sends a prospectus describing the book, he can probably recover his typing costs if the publisher asks to see the manuscript and then is negligent and loses it.

The prospectus is a written description of the manuscript, usually no more than four to eight pages in length. It should include a table of contents and give some general information about the scope of the book, the potential audience, other books in the field, some biographical information about the author, the approximate number of typewritten pages in the manuscript, and the date it will be available for submission to the publisher. When the manuscript is near completion, a prospectus should be prepared, with enough copies for those publishers listed in *The Literary Market Place* who might be interested in the book. The prospectus can be sent to a dozen or so publishers, inquiring if they desire to examine the final manuscript. When the manuscript is completed, the scholar will have a list of publishers who have expressed an interest in his book. In the meantime, field representatives of some of the publishers who received the prospectus may have called upon the scholar to discuss the book.

With sophisticated copying machines it is a simple matter to produce multiple copies of a manuscript, but the submission of the final manuscript to more than one publisher at a time, particularly without full disclosure of the fact, is contrary to accepted practice in the publishing world. Literary agents and most authors generally abide by this accepted practice. Many university presses will not look at a manuscript that is being considered elsewhere; the works of scholarship they consider must in most cases be submitted to expert referees for evaluation before acceptance can be proposed. "It is disconcerting," wrote Mark Carroll, Associate Director of Harvard University Press, "to invite an expert to read a manuscript, only to discover that he is already reading another copy for another publisher. Or to have expended time and effort to secure the necessary endorsements and then find that the author has signed an agreement the day before with another house. A final manuscript, produced by whatever technical means in however many copies, should be regarded as it was originally, a single entity, when it is ready for a publisher's attention." (Communication to the author, July 9, 1964.) Under certain exceptional circumstances, however, dictated by the nature of the work or by prior arrangement, some publishers will read a manuscript, though knowing it is being considered elsewhere concurrently. Some research organizations, for example, have "multiple-bidding" agreements with the publishers, in which case it is entirely proper for them to send copies of a final manuscript concurrently to all of the participating publishers.

Publishers seek the advice of other scholars in the field before they accept a manuscript for publication. They pay a fee to have the manuscript read critically, and frequently obtain two or more outside "readers' reports." These reports may or may not be shown to the author. In any case, the name of the reader is generally kept confidential. These readers' reports help the publisher to evaluate the manuscript and to decide whether to offer the author a contract for its publication. Princeton University Press asks their readers:

> Is this manuscript a significant contribution to the field?
>
> To what extent will it be useful to interested readers outside the particular field of scholarship? (Scholars in other fields, general readers, others?)
>
> Is the content an effective unit? Does it make a well-rounded book?
>
> Does the manuscript have a readable style? A distinguished style? Are stylistic revisions called for?
>
> If you were a publisher with a usually crowded schedule, would you consider this manuscript a worthy addition to your list? Is it something you would be proud to publish?
>
> Are there competing books in the field?
>
> Could the manuscript be improved by cutting? By expanding? Do you have recommendations for revisions?
>
> Do you recommend publication? Do you recommend publication provided the revisions suggested are satisfactorily made?

Scholars themselves thus act as advisors to publishers on which manuscripts should be published and thus help to decide what new literature will be added to their fields. A favorable reader's report from the leading scholar in the field can strongly influence a publisher's decision to accept the manuscript. In submitting a manuscript to a publisher, the author can suggest the names of possible readers—men who are knowledgeable about the subject; the publisher, of course, will make the final choice of readers.

Some publishers have a policy against reading dissertations unless they have been revised and edited for book publication. The manuscript may very well have satisfied the university's research and writing requirement for the degree, but still not be ready for publication as a book.

2. Kinds of Publication Agreements

There are four kinds of publication agreements used by book publishers:

Royalty agreement

This is the most common arrangement in use today. Under a royalty agreement, the author receives a percentage either of the list (retail) price of the book or of the publisher's net receipts from the sale of the book. (See Royalty, Section 3 of this chapter.) This is the most satisfactory arrangement for the publication of a scholarly book. If the book is a success and sells well, the author shares in its profits; if subsidiary rights in the book are sold, the author receives a share of these, too.

Sale of rights

Under this type of agreement, the author receives a fixed sum of money in return for assignment to the publisher of the copyright and all other rights and interests in the book. The publisher owns the book and retains all the profits from its sale, including the sale of subsidiary rights. This kind of publication agreement is not desirable if the book is expected to have a large sale and go through more than one edition or revision.

Stock-option agreements

In the case of new, small publishing houses, books are sometimes published under stock-option agreements or profit-sharing arrangements whereby the publisher compensates the author with shares of stock in the company. A certain number of shares of stock are given to the author at the time the contract is signed, and he has the right to purchase additional stock in the company at a reduced price.

Subsidy publishing agreements

Publishers who accept money from the authors of the books they publish are known in the trade as "vanity" publishing houses. The vanity publisher asks the author to pay the cost of production, in return for which he receives several hundred copies of the book and royalties on copies sold, sometimes as high as 40 to 80 per cent of the list price. Some publishers have been known to ask the scholar for a subsidy, even though they were prepared to go ahead and publish his book at their own expense.

Many fine books have been privately printed and then distributed by the authors themselves. If the market for a scholarly work is too small to be of interest to a commercial publisher or a university press, and if the scholar still wants his book published, he should consult *The Literary Market Place* for a list of commercial printers who work for the book trade. *The Literary Market Place* also lists free-lance promotion and advertising agents who will help with the distribution and sale of the book—all at the expense of the author, of course.

3. What the Publication Agreement Contains

An example of a book-publication agreement appears as Appendix F to this work. This is the contract signed by the author and the publisher setting forth the entire terms and conditions for the publication of the book, including the compensation that the author is to receive for his rights in the manuscript. The language used in publishers' contracts varies, but the principal provisions governing the legal rights and duties of the parties to the agreement include:

Grant of rights

The author grants to the publisher the full and exclusive right to publish and sell the book, and any revision thereof, throughout the world, in all countries and in all languages, under the publisher's own name and under other imprints or trade names, and the right to use the author's name and likeness or photograph in connection therewith wherever the book is published. This grant can be limited to book-publication rights only, and subsidiary rights, as discussed below, can be retained by the author or shared with the publisher.

Copyright

The author grants to the publisher the exclusive right to copyright the book, usually in the publisher's name in the United States and in the publisher's name or any other name in other countries. However, the copyright can just as well be in the author's name if the parties agree to it. The publisher should be obligated to apply for such copyright, either in his own name or in the name of the author, and to prepare the Registration Certificate and submit it to the Copyright Office. (See Chapter 6, Section 2.) Upon request from the publisher, the author contracts to do all acts necessary to effect and protect the book's copyright and any renewals thereof.

Delivery of manuscript

The author agrees to deliver the completed manuscript (in one or more copies as specified) to the publisher before a certain date. The manuscript must be in a form acceptable for typesetting and must contain approximately the number of words or typewritten pages specified in the contract. The author should notify the publisher in advance, in writing, if he is unable to meet the manuscript delivery date; publishers will usually extend the time by a letter amendment to the contract.

Advances

The publisher will sometimes advance an author a sum of money before his manuscript is completed. An *outright advance* is a bonus or free gift to the author on the signing of the contract. An *advance against royalties* is generally deducted from the author's first royalty checks. In the case of scholarly works, advances rarely exceed the costs of typing the manuscript, perhaps a few hundred dollars. If the scholar is an established writer, however, with previously published successful books, the publisher's advance may be several thousand dollars, generally paid one-third on the signing of the publication agreement, one-third on the delivery of the final manuscript to the publisher, and one-third on the publication of the book. If a manuscript is being sought after by several publishers, advances are likely to be more substantial. The amount of the advance and the conditions under which it will be paid to the author and repaid by him out of royalties to the publisher should be written into the publication agreement.

Author's warranty

The author warrants that he is the sole owner of the manuscript and has full power and authority to copyright it and to enter into the publication agreement. The author further warrants that the manuscript contains no libelous or unlawful material and that it in no way infringes upon any copyright or violates any right belonging to others. The author thus assumes full liability for any claim, demand, or suit brought against the publisher by reason of any material in the manuscript that violates the warranty, and agrees to hold the publisher harmless from all claims that he may sustain by reason of violation of the warranty. The author's warranty should be limited, if possible, by inserting language such as "so far as the author knows" he warrants that the manuscript contains no unlawful material; the author who has a good bargaining position with the publisher may also be able to include the words "by reason of a final judgment," thereby limiting his liability under the contract to successful suits in which there has been a court decision. Until suit or claim is settled, the publisher may withhold monies due the author from the sale of the book.

Options on future books

Some publishers ask that the author grant them an option to publish his next book. This contract provision is subject to negotiation, however, and many publishers today do not include it in their printed contract forms. Where the option does exist, the manuscript of the author's next book must be submitted to the publisher holding the option before it is sent elsewhere. The contract should read that the option expires unless the publisher has accepted the manuscript for publication within a certain number of days (sixty to ninety days) after he receives it.

Index

The author agrees to prepare a subject index for the book. Usually, it must be delivered to the publisher within two or three weeks after the author has received final page proofs. If the index is not so delivered, the publisher reserves the right to have it prepared by a professional indexer and to charge the expense of its preparation against the author's royalties. If the author does not want to index his book, he should endeavor to have the contract state that the publisher will supply the index at no expense to the author.

Artwork and miscellaneous items

The author agrees to furnish the publisher with complete and final copy for all illustrations that appear in the book, properly prepared for reproduction. As a practical matter, however, the publisher's art department usually assists the author in preparing the final drawings, illustrations, and other miscellaneous art items;

a list of free-lance artists, if needed, will be found in *The Literary Market Place*. The manuscript is to be complete, which means that it must include a title page, preface, foreword (if there is to be one), and table of contents. In the case of textbooks, the author agrees to prepare a teacher's manual or key if requested to do so by the publisher.

Publication date

Normally it takes about six to twelve months to publish a scholarly book. The publication time depends, however, on the length of the manuscript, the complexity of the typesetting required, and other production factors. Photo-offset books are generally published within three or four months after receipt of the camera-ready copy by the publisher. Although publishers' contracts for scholarly books do not normally state when the book will be published, the author may be able to negotiate this and have an approximate date included in the contract; the publisher, of course, reserves the right to determine when the book will actually be placed on sale, because seasonal timing is important for its proper promotion and advertising.

Quoted material

The author warrants that the manuscript contains no quoted material, including illustrations or drawings, from other copyrighted works without the other publishers' consent *and* the consent of the owner of such copyrighted material. Such consents must be in writing and the letters must be filed with the publisher. (See discussion of Fair Use, Chapter 7.)

Author's corrections

The author agrees to read the proofs for his book and to correct them. If he makes changes in the proofs—except for the correction of typesetter's errors—he is required to pay for such changes if they exceed a percentage (generally 10 per cent) of the original cost of composition. The costs of author's corrections are deducted from his first royalty payments.

Editing by the publisher

The publisher reserves the right to edit the manuscript for the original printing and for any reprinting, provided the meaning of the text is not materially altered. Changes made in the manuscript by a publisher's editors are subject to reasonable approval of the author. If the manuscript is on a highly technical subject, the contract should state that the author will see and approve the final copyedited manuscript before it is set in type.

Publishing details

The publisher reserves the right (1) to publish the book in a suitable format as to paper, printing, and binding; (2) to fix or alter the title and price; and (3) to use all customary means to market the book. Frequently, the price is not established until the publisher has set the book in type and has established his costs of production. The approximate price of the book, however, can be agreed on by the publisher and the author before the contract is signed, and any change in the price thereafter will be subject to the author's approval.

Author's complimentary copies

The publisher furnishes the author with a specific number of complimentary copies of the book, usually six. Additional copies of the book are sold to the author at the discount price agreed on in the contract. There is no limit on the number of copies of the book the author may purchase at the discount.

Revisions

The author agrees to revise the book, after it has been in print for a reasonable time, if the publisher considers this necessary and in the best interest of the work. The provisions of the original publishing agreement usually apply to revisions. If the author fails to provide a revision within a reasonable time after the publisher requests it, the publisher may have someone else prepare the revision and charge the cost of the work against the author's royalties. The revised work may also be as advertised in both the name of the original author and in the name of the person who makes the revision.

Out-of-print

When the publisher decides that the demand for the book no longer warrants its continued manufacture, he may allow it to go out-of-print and may destroy any or all of the plates, surplus books, or sheets without liability to the author. The contract should provide that all rights in an out-of-print book revert to the author. (See Section 6 below.)

Competing publications

The author agrees that, so long as the book is in print, he will not publish or furnish another publisher with any work on the same subject that conflicts with the sale of the book. This provision can be modified if the scholar is writing articles (and possibly another book) on the same subject; if the scholar is in a position to bargain with the publisher, the provision can be deleted altogether.

Payments

The publisher agrees to report on the sale of the book and to make payments to the author either annually or semiannually. With each report of sales, the publisher pays the author any balance due him. The publisher's report on sales will usually show the number of copies of the book sold, the list price or gross proceeds, the royalty percentage, and the amount of royalty enclosed.

Expense of publication

The manuscript is published entirely at the publisher's expense, and the author is not required to advance any sum whatever toward the costs of typesetting, printing, binding, or promotion or advertising of the book. If the author is required to pay any of the costs of publication, it is a subsidy arrangement. (See Section 2 above.)

Subsidiary rights

Subsidiary rights are generally not very important in the case of a scholarly or technical book; the income received from the sale of such rights is usually divided equally between the author and the publisher. The subsidiary rights to a book may include:

1. Theatrical Motion Picture,
2. Television (live and motion picture),
3. Radio,
4. Stage,
5. Recordings,
6. Translations,
7. Abridgments, Digests, or Condensations,
8. Serialization,
9. Book Club Rights,
10. Foreign Editions in English Language,
11. Reprint Edition by another Publisher,
12. Anthology,
13. Microfilm and Microcard Editions, and
14. Advertising and Commercial Uses.

It is possible for the scholar to negotiate separately with the publisher for any subsidary right that is valuable, and it can be expressly excluded from the contract, thereby belonging to the scholar.

Royalty

The royalty paid to the author is computed either as a percentage of the price at which the book is sold or as a percentage of the publisher's total volume of sales of the book. The first is called a royalty based on *list price,* the second a royalty based on *net receipts.* Because publishers' net receipts vary, depending on their discounts to booksellers, the author should inquire about the publisher's discounts before signing a net-receipts contract. It is not uncommon for a straight royalty of 10 or 15 per cent of net receipts to be paid by publishers on scholarly books, but a sliding scale is sometimes used, namely, 10 per cent of net receipts on the first 3,500 copies sold, 12½ per cent on the next 3,500 copies sold, and 15 per cent thereafter. (See also Chapter 2, Section 4.) Some publishers make a distinction between the royalties they pay on copies of the regular trade edition sold in the United States and all other copies sold; lesser royalties are applied to books and sheets sold for export, paperback editions, mail order sales, and so forth.

Although the royalty is important to the author, it is well to remember that the money from the sale of a book must cover the cost of producing the book, the advertising and promotional outlay, and the profit to the publisher as well as the author's royalty. If the royalty is too high, the promotion and advertising of the book is likely to suffer.

Incapacity of the author

The authorship of a book is a personal undertaking. It is of such personal character that it normally can be performed only by a particular person. The physical incapacity of the author before the book is completed, therefore, will normally excuse him from legal liability under the publishing contract. The defense of the author in such cases is that unforeseen circumstances, that is, physical incapacity to complete the writing of the book, render it impossible for him to fulfill his contractual obligation to the publisher.

Default of the publisher

If the publisher fails to live up to his contractual commitments for publication of the book—for example, if he fails to proceed with the typesetting and production of the book within a reasonable time after receipt of the final, edited copy of the manuscript, and if the delay is not due to circumstances beyond his control—then the publisher may have defaulted under the contract and the contract might be cancellable by the author. It is unwise, however, for an author to attempt to cancel a book-publishing contract, even if there has been unreasonable delay in the production of the book, without first consulting an attorney who will advise him as to his rights and obligations under the contract.

Assignment

The right to personal service under a publishing contract is not assignable by either party, unless the contract expressly provides otherwise. Some publishers' printed contracts are assignable, others are not. Ideally, the scholar's book-publication contract should provide that no assignment is binding on either party without the written consent of the other.

4. Marketing the Book

Most publishers take pride in the thoroughness with which they market their books. They have an advertising and promotion department that concerns itself exclusively with the sale of books through bookstores, by mail order, through field travelers, and so forth. The marketing facilities and selling experience of publishers vary greatly. Some publicize their books almost entirely by mail, others have a large staff of travelers continually calling on bookstores and promoting the sale of their books.

If the scholar's book is intended for general readership, it is a *trade book*, namely, a book sold primarily through the bookstores and of interest to almost everybody, not limited to a specialized audience, as is a scientific work, a reference book, or a textbook. Novels, short stories, poetry, and some nonfiction are trade books and are promoted by the publishers' trade departments; business books, school and college textbooks, reference works, scientific texts, and juveniles are generally promoted by separate departments which the publishers have set up for this purpose.

There are several ways in which the author can assist the publisher's promotion department in marketing his book. The author knows the book better than anyone else, and he knows the audience for which it was written. He can provide the raw material from which the publisher's advertising department will write promotional blurbs, brochures, the book's jacket copy, or advertisements for professional journals. He can recommend scholarly periodicals and learned journals in which the book should be reviewed or advertised, and he can compile lists of persons who should receive the promotional brochure. In planning a promotion and advertising campaign for a new book, most publishers welcome the assistance of the author, and within the limits of the financial budget allotted for the book, they try to meet his requests for advertisements, reviews, and notices in particular professional journals, newspapers, and other important sources of publicity.

5. Endorsement of a Book

Complimentary advance copies of new books are sent to scholars by publishers for the purpose of review and to obtain comments about the book for their promotional and advertising materials. In asking for an endorsement of a new book, some publishers have a printed form on which the comment is to be written, with a space to be checked indicating whether the comment may be used in advertising materials. A publisher cannot legally quote from a letter endorsing a new book, either on the jacket of a book or in promotional materials, without the letter writer's permission. There have been cases in which publishers have included a statement from a scholar about a book in their promotional brochures without first securing permission. A letter to the publisher objecting to the quotation is generally all that is required to have it removed from the brochure.

6. Out-of-Print Books

When the book's sales begin to decline sharply the publisher may decide to "remainder" it, that is, to offer the book for sale at a fraction of the original price. Thereafter, when the publisher's supply of the book is exhausted, he may declare it to be out-of-print. The legal rights revert to the author, if the contract so provides, and the author may then seek a reprint publisher for his book (generally a paperback house). Some publishers allow a book to go out-of-print when the sales fall below two hundred copies a year; they transfer the rights in the book to the author and offer him an opportunity to purchase the plates of the book at fair value. Out-of-print books are placed with reprint publishers either for a flat fee or on a royalty basis.

5

Protecting rights
in the work—copyright

1. A Historical Sketch

Although it can be (and has been) argued that the right of an
author to his creation is an inherent and natural right, the statement is more an expression of political or social philosophy than
a deduction from historical or legal evidence. Evidence of the early
existence of copyright as we understand it is weak. Among certain
primitive peoples, rights in formulas and rituals are recognized, and
perhaps such notions are the ancestors of copyright. Literary
property did not exist in ancient Greece; there was free borrowing
from other authors. Nor were the rights of authors recognized in
ancient Rome. Occasionally monasteries became famous for their
particular manuscript copy of a famous work and would not permit
copies to be made, or would permit the privilege only upon payment. This is not protection of the author's right, however, but protection exercised by the owner of a physical object.

There is a story often told that Saint Columba sat up all night
making a copy of Abbot Finnian's Psalter. When the Abbot learned
of it, he demanded the copy Columba had made. Columba refused and the question was referred to King Diarmid in his palace

at Tara. Diarmid, in the year A.D. 567, gave judgment for the good Abbot, saying "to every cow her calf, and accordingly to every book its copy." Despite this precedent (if it is fact rather than fiction), it does not appear that there was any statute or common law or custom that protected a literary work and gave the author the right to control its duplication.

The invention of printing, making possible more extensive duplication of books, changed the picture.

In Venice, John of Spira was given in 1469 the exclusive right for five years to print the Epistles of Cicero and of Pliny. In 1486 the Senate of Venice gave to Antonio Sabellico the exclusive privilege to print his work *Decades Rerum Venetiarum*, and in 1491 Venice gave to Peter of Ravenna and the printer of his choice the exclusive right to print and sell his *Phoenix*. These may be the first recorded instances of a grant of copyright to an author. Most of the Venetian privileges were grants to printer-publishers rather than to authors.

In 1476 Caxton established his press at Westminster. Between 1476 and 1710 there were various events, proclamations, decrees, and laws relating to the development of copyright. As books became more common and the power of the printed word more apparent, Crown and Church became concerned and efforts were made to control printing. Royal privileges were granted to printers. In 1557 the Stationers' Company was founded for the purpose of regulating the press. From the point of view of the King, this was an opportunity to control printing. From the point of view of the Stationers it was a union for their economic betterment. In 1710 the first copyright statute was adopted by Parliament. It was called An Act for the Encouragement of Learning. For a discussion of this statute and the events leading to its adoption, see *The First Copyright Statute* by Harry Ransom (Austin: University of Texas Press, 1956).

In France the edict of Moulins in 1566 prohibited the printing of any book without permission of the King and a grant of letters of privilege. In both France and England the history of copyright is intertwined with the history of censorship. The famous 1637 decree of the Star Chamber concerning printing prohibited the printing of any book unless it were licensed.

In the United States, Connecticut and Massachusetts passed copyright acts in 1783 granting copyright protection for twenty-one years. Virginia passed a similar law in 1785, and New York and New Jersey followed suit in 1786. The first United States Copyright Act was passed in 1790; it granted protection for fourteen years, with the possibility of renewal for another fourteen years if the author were still alive.

A thorough legal history of copyright has not yet been written. For the scholar interested in pursuing the history of copyright and literary property, a selected list of references is included in Appendix H.

2. The Constitutional Basis

The United States Copyright Act finds its constitutional basis in Article I, Section 8, Clause 8, which states that Congress shall have power "To promote the progress of science and useful arts by securing for limited times to authors and inventors the exclusive rights to their respective writings and discoveries." Despite the language used, it is not necessary to show that a literary or artistic work does serve "to promote the progress of science and useful arts" in order for it to be eligible for copyright. It is the fact that authors can secure financial and other rewards for their creative activities that help to promote such progress. The word "writings" as used in the constitutional provision has been broadly interpreted to include such things as engravings, maps, sculpture, and motion pictures.

3. The Rights Protected by Copyright

What are the rights which a statutory copyright gives to the copyright owner? The broadest right is that stated in Section 1 (a) of the Copyright Act: "To print, reprint, publish, copy and vend the copyrighted work." The meaning of these rights is generally clear, although the question of whether or not the allegedly infringing work is a copy has presented the courts with difficult problems. The question may be whether there is sufficient similarity between two stories or two paintings, or whether a reproduction in another medium, such as a photograph of a piece of sculpture or a three-dimensional reproduction of a cartoon, is a copy. It must be remembered that copyright protects only against copying, not against similarity based on an independent conception or arising out of use of the same public domain sources. The entire subject of infringement is complex and beyond the scope of this work. In the event of a suspected infringement, the scholar will wish to consult a lawyer versed in copyright matters.

The right to vend is the right to the first sale of any copy. Once the copyright proprietor has disposed of copies of a copyrighted work, he cannot impose conditions upon their resale. For example, an author cannot prevent a secondhand book store from selling his works at a price he deems less than their real worth.

Among other rights of the copyright owner are the rights to translate the copyrighted work; to make other versions of it; to turn it into a play, novel, or other dramatic work; to arrange or adapt it if it is a musical work; to deliver, authorize the delivery of, read, or present the copyrighted work in public for profit if it is a lecture or similar production or other nondramatic literary work; to perform the work publicly if it is a play; to perform it publicly for profit if it is a musical composition.

4. Moral Right

Although moral right, or *droit moral,* is not mentioned in the Copyright Act, it is recognized by the law of some countries. This is, broadly, the right of an author to be identified with his work (and, conversely, not to be named as the author of a work he did not write) and to prevent its mutilation and distortion. It has been stated in a number of judicial opinions that the United States does not recognize an author's moral right, but if a court is so disposed it can read into a contract an implied provision to achieve the necessary end—for example, a provision that the author shall be entitled to authorship credit whenever the work is printed or otherwise reproduced, or that no changes in the work may be made without the prior consent of the author. Occasionally the courts in the United States will use other areas of the law, such as the law of defamation, unfair competition, or right of privacy, to achieve a just result in a particular case. It has been stated by at least one expert that although the label "moral right" is not used by the American courts, they do in general arrive at much the same results as European courts.

6

How to obtain statutory copyright

1. The Copyright Notice

It is frequently thought that copyright is secured by "sending something to Washington" or by registering something somewhere. Before publication, literary, musical, and artistic works are protected by the common law copyright. (See Chapter 3.) Statutory copyright is obtained (with the exceptions noted in Chapter 3, Section 4) by *publishing the work with a proper copyright notice.* The word "publishing" has a special meaning in copyright law. (See Chapter 3, Section 2.) When the work has been published with the proper notice it is then protected by United States copyright.

The notice requirement has been strictly construed in the past, although some tendency toward leniency where there has been a substantial compliance has been indicated by some recent decisions. The statutory provision reads:

> The notice of copyright required by section 10 of this title shall consist either of the word "Copyright," the abbreviation "Copr.," or the symbol ©, accompanied by the name of the copyright proprietor, and if the work be a printed literary, musical, or dramatic work, the notice shall include also the year in which the copyright was secured by publication.

Note that there are three elements to the proper notice:

(1) The word "Copyright" or "Copr.," or the symbol ©.

(2) The name of the copyright proprietor.

(3) The year in which the work was first published, if it is a printed literary, musical, or dramatic work.

(1) The © is necessary to obtain protection under the Universal Copyright Convention, which has now been adhered to by most of the major countries of the world, including the United States, Canada, England, France, Germany, and Japan. A list of subscribing countries appears in Appendix D. For whatever psychological effect it may have on a potential infringer unfamiliar with the © symbol, the word copyright and the © are frequently used together. If the work is first published abroad, it should also contain a complete copyright notice using the symbol ©.

(2) The name in the notice must be the name of the copyright proprietor. If the person whose name appears in the notice is not the copyright proprietor, the notice is inadequate and the work falls into the public domain. If, for example, a publication agreement grants all rights in a literary work to the publisher, then the name in the copyright notice should be that of the publisher. If, on the other hand, the publishing agreement is only a license to publish the work, then the copyright notice should be in the name of the author. If the copyright is transferred to another person, the name of that other person may be substituted in the copyright notice on future printings of the work, but this can be done *only after* the recordation in the Copyright Office of a written assignment of the copyright. One author of a joint enterprise may secure the copyright in his own name and hold it in trust for the benefit of his co-author or co-authors. The notice may use the pen name or pseudonym of the author, if this is the author's wish.

(3) The year in the notice must be the year of the first publication of the work. Reprints of the work and new editions should continue to use the original year in the notice. If new material is added to a new edition, both years should appear in the notice. For example, if a work were originally published in 1957, a proper form of copyright notice would be: © 1957 by Schuyler Scholar. If the book is printed in 1965 in a new edition with revisions and other new material, the copyright notice should read: © 1957, 1965 by Schuyler Scholar. If the new material is by a person different from the original author, the notice should be in the following

form: © 1957 by Schuyler Scholar, © 1965 by Scott Scholar. If the year contained in the notice is the year before the year in which the work is actually published (for example, if the publication was scheduled for December, 1964 and the book was not actually published until January, 1965) the variance has been held not to forfeit the copyright. The twenty-eight year copyright term begins to run in such a case on the last day of the year used in the notice. However, if the year date in the notice is 1965 and the book was actually published in 1964, the variance from proper notice may possibly be fatal and cause a forfeiture of the copyright.

Where a work has been substantially rewritten so as to constitute a new work for purposes of the Copyright Act, it may contain the year of the revised publication without the earlier year. Such a practice may be dangerous, however, and is not recommended.

For maps, works of art, reproductions of works of art, drawings, sculpture and photographs, a slightly different form of notice is permitted. The notice may on such works be the same as on a book, or it may consist of the symbol © accompanied by the initial or symbol of the copyright proprietor, provided that the full name of the copyright proprietor appears on some accessible portion of the copies or of the margin, back, permanent base or pedestal, or of the substance on which the copies are mounted. The year need not appear insofar as United States copyright is concerned, but in order to qualify for protection under the Universal Copyright Convention, the year of first publication must also appear in the notice.

The copyright notice must not only contain the required elements, but must also be in the prescribed place. Section 20 of the Copyright Act states:

> The notice of copyright shall be applied, in the case of a book or other printed publication, upon its title page or the page immediately following, or if a periodical either upon the title page or upon the first page of text of each separate number or under the title heading, or if a musical work either upon its title page or the first page of music.

In situations where it is difficult to determine which page is the title page, the copyright notice may generally be placed on the front cover or on the first leaf immediately following the cover.

The importance of the notice cannot be overemphasized. It is absolutely crucial to obtaining copyright. The law does provide:

> Where the copyright proprietor has sought to comply with the
> provisions of this title with respect to notice, the omission by acci-
> dent or mistake of the prescribed notice from a particular copy or
> copies shall not invalidate the copyright. . . .

This clause will not save the copyright if all of the copies of the work
do not contain a notice or if the notice is omitted through an over-
sight or through a mistaken notion of what the law is on the subject. It appears to be primarily intended to protect the copyright
where some of the copies of a work through accident or mistake
do not bear the notice. Absence of the notice even in these situations does prevent recovery of damages against an innocent infringer who has been misled by the absence of the notice. The most
delightful "nonnotice" of which the authors are aware appears in the
revised edition of J. Frank Dobie's *Guide to Life and Literature of
the Southwest:*

> Not copyright in 1942
> Again not copyright in 1952
> Anybody is welcome to help himself to any
> of it in any way.

2. Registration

It was once the law in the United States that a work fell into
the public domain if copies were not deposited in the Copyright
Office not later than the day of its publication. This has not been
the law since 1909. The deposit of copies in Washington and the
registration of the work are no longer conditions for obtaining copyright. The statute does provide that there shall be "promptly" deposited in the Copyright Office two complete copies of the best
edition of the work after it has been copyrighted by publication
with the proper notice. The word "promptly" is not defined in the
statute, and court decisions have emptied the word of meaning.
Registration and deposit at any time during the original copyright
term is probably sufficient. The Register of Copyrights can, however, demand the deposit of copies. (The man holding this office
is called the Regist*er*, not the Regist*rar*.)
Registration and deposit are a prerequisite for filing suit on a

copyright, and the sensible procedure is to comply with the law promptly after publication so that the matter is not overlooked. The procedure is simple. The appropriate form, two complete copies of the best edition of the work, and the fee of $4.00 are sent to the Register of Copyrights. A part of the application form is returned with the seal of the Copyright Office affixed; this is the certificate of registration. When mailing the application and copies to the Copyright Office, no postage need be paid. A reproduction of the form for registration of the copyright in a book appears as Appendix C.

Normally registration is taken care of by the publisher and not by the individual author. If the author wishes to register a work for copyright, instructions and copies of the applicable form can be obtained from the Register of Copyrights, Library of Congress, Washington, D.C. 20540.

3. Duration and Renewal

The present Copyright Act provides for an original copyright term of twenty-eight years from the date of first publication of the work. If a work has been copyrighted as an unpublished work (See Chapter 3, Section 4), it is the date of the original deposit in the Copyright Office that begins the copyright term, not the date of any subsequent publication. The copyright may be renewed by persons specified in the Act for a second term of twenty-eight years. Before publication, copyright protection depends on state law and continues forever if the work remains unpublished.

In most foreign countries copyright begins upon creation of the work (as is the case with the common law copyright), and the term of protection continues for the life of the author and for a certain number of years (usually fifty) after his death. These countries do not have the dual system of copyright protection which is a cardinal feature of the American law of literary property. The possibility of a change in United States law to conform with the general law of foreign countries has been much discussed in copyright circles. Pending possible copyright law revision, Congress enacted a law in 1962 to the effect that any renewal term of a copyright that would otherwise have expired between September 19, 1962 and December 31, 1965 is automatically continued in force until December 31, 1965. (See Chapter 9.) Some foreign countries adopted legislation after World War II extending the term of all copyrights in effect at the beginning of the war by a period equal to the duration of the war.

The copyright in a work may be renewed by the author if he is alive in the twenty-eighth year of the copyright term; if the author is not then living, it may be renewed by his widow or children, or if there are no widow or children, then by his executor, or if he left no will, by his next of kin. In certain cases the copyright may be renewed by the owner of the copyright at the time of renewal. This is so where the work was first published after the author's death; where the work is a periodical or other composite work (See Section 6 below); where the work was copyrighted by an employer for whom the work was made for hire (See Section 7 below); and where the work was copyrighted by a corporation otherwise than as the assignee or licensee of the individual author.

If the scholar has published a work in a periodical or in a symposium volume or other composite work, he may make a separate *renewal* registration whether the work was copyrighted separately or as part of the work in which it appeared.

If an author assigns a copyright to a publisher, motion picture producer, or other user, he will normally be asked to assign the copyright for both the original term of twenty-eight years and the renewal term. The author can make such an assignment, but it is effective only if he survives to the twenty-eighth year of the copyright term. If he dies before this time, his widow or children are the proper parties to renew the copyright, and his assignment of the renewal term is not binding upon them (unless the user had the foresight to obtain their separate agreement at the time of the original transaction). The user would have to negotiate a new agreement with the widow or other proper party if he desired to continue to use the work.

The Copyright Act does not state the form of notice required on a work in which the copyright has been renewed. It is recommended that the original notice be retained and that a reference to the renewal be added. For example: Copyright 1937 by Schuyler Scholar / Copyright renewed 1965 by Sophie Scholar.

4. Assignment

A copyright may be transferred. Transfer of a copyright requires an instrument in writing clearly setting forth the intention of the parties. It should be recorded in the Copyright Office within three months after its execution if it was executed within the United States, or within six months of its execution if it was executed abroad. Failure to record the assignment within these time limits does not invalidate the assignment as between the parties, but it does void the assignment as against any subsequent purchaser who pays a valuable consideration for the copyright, who does not know about the prior assignment, and who does record his assignment. The original signed instrument should be sent to the Copyright Office for recording with the fee of $3.00. It will be photocopied and returned.

Change of the name which appears in the copyright notice after a transfer of ownership is discussed in Section 1 of this Chapter.

5. New Editions and Revisions

The principal point to be made in connection with a new edition or revision is that it may require a change in the copyright notice in order to protect the new matter. The subject is discussed in Section 1 of this Chapter.

6. Joint and Composite Works

Not infrequently the scholar will collaborate with other scholars in the writing of a single work; this is a *joint* work, and the authors will be joint owners of the copyright. The scholar may also contribute a chapter or chapters to a book consisting of chapter contributions by various authors under the general editorship of one person. This is a *composite* work, and under such circumstances the work may be copyrighted in the names of the authors, or in the name of one of the authors, the editor, or the publisher, who can hold the copyright in trust for all of the authors, preferably by virtue of a written agreement among them. If the work is a composite and not a joint work, it would also be possible to copyright separately each of the individual contributions. To do so, the proper copyright notice must appear on the first page of each individual contribution. Absent such specific copyright notice for each contribution, the copyright of the entire work protects all of its component parts. One co-owner may use or license the use of the work without the consent of the others, but he must account to them for their share of any profits which he derives from such license to a third party, and may even be required to account if he makes use of the work himself.

7. Employment for Hire

The scholar may write a book or article as part of his duties while employed by a corporation, or he may have been commissioned to write a particular work. Under the Copyright Act, the employer in such circumstances is deemed the "author" of the work for copyright purposes. This is sometimes referred to as the "employment for hire" doctrine. This result can be varied by the contract between the parties, and the employer and employee are free to contract that the employee is the owner of the copyright even though the work is written for hire. The law is not clear on whether an assignment from the employer to his employee apart from the contract itself is necessary under such circumstances.

8. Ghostwriters

The question of who is entitled to the copyright when a "ghost" is employed by a celebrity to write an article or a book should be

settled by the contract between the parties. Under the employment-for-hire doctrine, the employer would presumably be entitled
to the copyright in the absence of an agreement to the contrary,
but the answer is not certain, and there are British decisions to
the effect that if the ghost did the actual writing, he is the author
and is entitled to the copyright.

7

Using the work of others—fair use

The copyright law serves to protect the work of the scholar against theft by others, but it is also a potential barrier to the scholar's freedom to use the work of others. The scholar may wish to use the copyrighted work of others in various ways. The simplest use is for purposes of research. Such general use is of course not a violation of the copyright. The scholar who publishes intends that others coming after him shall use his work; this is the way in which knowledge grows. Inevitably the work of the scholar builds upon the work of his contemporaries and of those who have gone before him. The ideas and theories of earlier scholars are not protected by copyright.

What about making copies? It is probably safe to say that the scholar may copy by hand for his personal use sections of a copyrighted work without infringing the copyright. May he make photocopies for his personal use? Probably, but see the discussion of photocopying of copyrighted work in Chapter 10.

Is the scholar free to quote from a copyrighted work, and, if so, how much may he quote? The Copyright Act does not answer or even address itself to this question, but the courts have developed the doctrine of *fair use*, which is intended to permit the reasonable use of copyrighted material and to mediate between the conflicting interests involved.

The problem arising from these conflicting interests was early stated by Lord Mansfield in an English case decided in 1785:

> . . . we must take care to guard against two extremes equally prejudicial; the one, that men of ability, who have employed their time for the service of the community, may not be deprived of their just merits, and the reward of their ingenuity, and labour; the other, that the world may not be deprived of improvements, nor the progress of the arts be retarded.

It is not always easy to decide whether a particular use is a fair use or an infringement of copyright. In a case in which Learned and Augustus Hand were two of the three judges on the court, the court said: "the issue of fair use . . . is the most troublesome in the whole law of copyright." The scholar should not therefore expect to solve all the fair use problems which may confront him simply because he has this book at hand.

Here are some cases which have vexed the courts in connection with determining whether a particular use is a fair use or an infringement of copyright:

(1) Two characters in a magazine story hear a song over the radio. Ten lines of the song are quoted. Held a fair use.

(2) Three sentences from a book on the human voice are quoted in an advertising pamphlet for cigarettes. Held not a fair use.

(3) A book on the history of American popular songs sets out the words to a song, giving credit for its authorship. Held not a fair use.

(4) A novel based on the life of Hans Christian Andersen contains specific passages from a biography of Andersen and acknowledges the use made of the biography in writing the novel; certain concepts and ideas which were original with the author of the biography are used by the novelist; the biographer has based her material on years of research in original source materials in Danish. Held not a fair use.

(5) The author of a book called *Scientific Physiognomy—How to Read Faces* consulted in its preparation a number of works in the field. The author of one of those works sued. Held a fair use.

(6) A numerical telephone directory was issued, based on the regular telephone directory but containing the numbers under each exchange in order; the subscriber's name followed the number. The telephone company filed suit. Held not a fair use.

(7) The American Institute of Architects issued a booklet containing forms for agreements between architects, owners, contractors, and other parties. An architect made and used six copies of one of the most important forms in the booklet, delivering them to the

owner and contractor with whom he was dealing. The Institute sued for infringement of its copyright in the booklet. Held a fair use.

The key criteria which the courts have considered in fair use cases are: the type of use involved, the amount of material used and its relative value, and the extent to which the use may prejudice the sale or diminish the need for the original work.

Fortunately, the use which is apt to be looked upon with the most favor by the courts is the use of quotations by a scholar in a scholarly work. The scholar may wish to illustrate a particular point of view with the words of someone holding that view, or he may wish to use language which extraordinarily well sums up or expresses a particular view or position. He may use the quotation as a source, showing the authority for his further conclusions, or he may set forth the quotation in order to criticize or differ with it. The doctrine of fair use is much more likely to be found applicable with respect to these kinds of uses.

Quotation for purposes of review and criticism is generally acknowledged to be within the scope of the fair use doctrine. There seem to be no reported American cases in which the author has claimed that a quotation in a review or critical article constituted infringement of his copyright.

If the quotation is for any of the legitimate purposes mentioned above, it is important that the scholar is using the quotation in an independent work. He will not be permitted to quote simply because he has concluded that the material is useful; if the fair use doctrine is to apply, the quotation should be used in a work involving creative effort on his part.

A scholarly motive and the exercise of creative talent are not enough, however. In every case, the courts will consider all of the relevant criteria in determining whether the use is reasonable. An important criterion is, of course, the amount of material used and its relative value. There is no fixed rule as to the number of words which can be quoted without infringing a copyright, although one frequently hears that fifty or one hundred or three hundred words or four bars or eight bars of music may be quoted without permission. There is absolutely no basis in the law for these supposed rules, and under the proper circumstances, the use of twenty words or one bar of music may be sufficient to constitute copyright infringement and render the user liable for damages. The length of the material quoted must be considered in connection with its relative value in the work quoted from. Quoting six lines from a twelve-line poem involves the use of a substantial part of the work, whereas the use of twelve lines from a three-hundred-page work is probably not substantial. If the result of research covered in five hundred pages is boiled down to a one-page chart, reproduction of the chart may well not be protected by the fair use doctrine. If, on the other hand, the author of a work sums up his position in one paragraph, quoting the paragraph would probably be a fair use. Quoting a list or compilation may be an infringement. The scholar should make his own independent listing, although he may use the other material as a means of verification or a checklist.

It must be emphasized that all relevant factors must be considered together, and the scholar cannot decide whether it is necessary to ask permission without considering all of the factors: the type of use, the amount of material quoted and its relative value, and the effect on the original work. If the proposed use can be in effect a substitute for the original work, the court is unlikely to uphold the defense of fair use. The quotation of an entire poem or short story in an anthology is likely to impair the sale or diminish the need for the original work. Mimeographing an article for members of a class or for a group of employees is direct competition with the original work. If the copyright owner were to file suit, the court would probably find that such a use constituted an infringement of the copyright and not a fair use. Certainly the reproduction of all or a substantial part of a work diminishes the need for the original. Presenting an entire work in an anthology or compilation requires that permission from the copyright owner be obtained, and the scholar should follow this practice assiduously.

The practical problem facing the scholar who desires to quote from a work is whether he should seek permission? Since his proposed work may contain quotations from a large number of books, with different publishers, obtaining permission is frequently a formidable task adding to the difficulties of writing a scholarly work. And the possibility always exists that permission may be refused or a fee exacted, even though the proposed use is clearly a fair use.

If the scholar has a contract for publication of a book, it will usually contain a clause in which he guarantees that he has not used copyrighted materials in the manuscript in a way which will infringe the rights of the copyright owner; sometimes the contract will provide that he has not used copyrighted materials without the written permission of the copyright owner. The publisher may require that permission letters from copyright owners of work quoted must be filed at the time the contract is signed. The position taken by his publisher may determine whether or not the scholar will ask for permission to quote the materials he is using.

Most publishers have a policy relating to the amount of materials which may be used from works which they control, but some do not have any fixed rule. The amounts which publishers consider appropriate vary from four short sentences or thirty words up to five hundred words. With respect to any quotation longer than the specified limit, which, as indicated, may vary considerably, permission is required. Of course, if the entire work consists of five hundred words or less, this general rule does not apply. The same thing is true with respect to poetry, where if two lines constitute a complete stanza, for example, or if the quotation is an otherwise complete unit, permission is required. Generally a publisher will aggregate all quotations from a particular work for purposes of making the foregoing computation.

The scholar may ask how a publisher can fix the amount of material which can be quoted when the doctrine of fair use establishes no fixed amount of material which may be used. The answer is that the policy of the publisher is not binding as a matter of law, and although a publisher requires permission for all quotations over thirty words, a seventy-five-word quotation may under the circumstances be a fair use. The safe approach, when in doubt, is to ask for permission. In asking for permission, the publisher should be given the title of the book, the author, the length of the selection involved (including the pages and the lines to be quoted), and the name and type of work in which the quotation is to be used. If the scholar's work will be published outside of the United States, care should be taken that the grant of permission is sufficiently broad.

Some publishers make a distinction between a quotation used for purposes of illustration or for the citing of authority and quotations which are presented as primary material for their own sake, as in anthologies or books of readings. If such a distinction is made, permission is always required for the latter type of use. Most publishers require that full credit be given to the author and to the publisher. A few charge a fee for quotations over a particular length. One publisher makes a charge of $10 for two hundred words and $25 for five hundred words. The publishers of the scholar's work may themselves have a policy with respect to length of quotations for which they will require permission of the copyright owner. The scholar may be saved considerable labor if he can ascertain this before he signs his contract.

In order to facilitate the use by scholars of copyrighted materials where the need is legitimate, most members of the Association of American University Presses have adopted a policy concerning permissions. Omitting the preamble, the Resolution reads as follows:

(1) That publications issued under our imprints may be quoted without specific prior permission in works of original scholarship for accurate citation of authority or for criticism, review, or evaluation, subject to the conditions listed below.

(2) That appropriate credit be given in the case of each quotation.

(3) That waiver of the requirement for specific permission does not extend to quotations that are complete units in themselves (as poems, letters, short stories, essays, journal articles, complete chapters or sections of books, maps, charts, graphs, tables, drawings, or other illustrative materials), in whatever form they may be reproduced, nor does the waiver extend to quotation of whatever length presented as primary material for its own sake (as in anthologies or books of readings).

(4) The fact that specific permission for quoting of material may be waived under this agreement does not relieve the quoting author and publisher from the responsibility of determining fair use of such material.

The scholar can be guided accordingly if the work he wishes to quote from is published by one of the signatory presses. A list of the signatories appears as Appendix E.

In a letter to the editor of *Publisher's Weekly*, printed in the April 25, 1960 issue, a representative of a distinguished English publishing house, Routledge and Kegan Paul, Ltd., wrote:

> The Ph.D. season is with us again, and I am bombarded by letters from aspirants all over the United States of America asking for permission to quote trivial short passages from various books which we have published in the past fifteen years or more, either in their Ph.D. theses, which will be microfilmed, or in various publications of university presses or even commercial publishers.
>
> The British Publisher's Association entered into an agreement with the Society of Authors to the effect that short passages from copyright work may be used in the course of criticism without permission being obtained from the publisher whose work is being quoted, if the passage is less than three hundred words long.

Suppose a work being used by the scholar contains a quotation from an earlier work, a copy of which the scholar is unable to locate, but the scholar wishes to use the same quotation. The better procedure would be to check the original work if possible; if not, the use of the quotation is subject to the general rules of fair use. If the quotation is from a work still protected by copyright, the first user may have received permission from the copyright owner. The fact that he used the quotation does not mean that subsequent users can automatically make use of it. Because publication under the fair use doctrine would not cause the quoted portion to fall into the public domain, brief quotations do not require a copyright notice. When the quotation is substantial, and remember that the word "substantial" is relative, it is the better practice, and is sometimes required by the publisher, that a footnote on the page where the quotation appears should contain the copyright notice of the quoted work.

What if the quotation in question is a translation? In that case the translation is independently copyrightable (See Chapter 8, Section 4), and the scholar should go back to the original source and make his own translation, if possible. Use of the translation is still subject to the doctrine of fair use, however.

The operation of the doctrine of fair use cannot be prevented by the wishes of the author. The statement frequently seen near the copyright notice—"No one may quote from this work without the written permission of the publisher"—is wholly ineffective. The legend does usually contain the further statement that brief extracts for purposes of a review may be made, but the scholar has the right to make a fair use of copyrighted material notwithstanding any prohibition to the contrary which may appear in the work.

8

Some special categories

1. Letters and Diaries

Letters and diaries are usually unpublished and therefore are subject to the common law copyright of the writer. (See Chapter 3 for a discussion of copyright in unpublished works.) The distinction between the intangible copyright and the tangible object is important in the case of letters. The ownership of a letter (that is, the paper on which it is written) lies with the recipient, who may destroy the letter or otherwise dispose of it. The right of publication is retained by the writer. Obviously, then, the scholar wishing to publish letters or include selections from letters in a projected work must obtain the consent of two persons. First, he must obtain the consent of the owner of the letter in order to have physical access to it; second, he must obtain the consent of the writer or his heirs in order to copy and publish it. Obvious difficulties present themselves in tracing the proper copyright owners with respect to letters whose authors have long since been dead. Here the scholar must weigh the practicalities and obtain such competent advice as he can. Where it is impossible to trace the ownership, courts would undoubtedly be lenient in applying the doctrine of fair use.

Diaries present a similar problem. The scholar may be able to consult a diary that has been given to a library or other public institution, but the right to make copies of the diary may rest with the heirs of the diary writer. Investigation must be made of the circumstances under which the library acquired the diary. Perhaps the terms of the gift included the right to publish, if the donor did in fact have that right. (See Chapter 3, Section 2.)

2. Government Publications

Government publications are not subject to copyright. (See Chapter 11, Section 5.) Section 8 of the Copyright Act states that "No copyright shall subsist . . . in any publication of the United States Government, or any reprint, in whole or in part, thereof. . . ." (There is an exception with respect to black-and-white illustrations of United States postage stamps printed as a public document to be sold by the Superintendent of Documents, which may be copyrighted by the Postmaster General.) The scholar is therefore free to quote from government publications without permission, except as noted below.

The Act goes on to say that:

> The publication or reproduction by the Government, either separately or in a public document, of any material in which copyright is subsisting shall not be taken to cause any abridgement or annulment of the copyright or to authorize any use or appropriation of such copyright material without the consent of the copyright proprietor.

Therefore government publication of copyrighted material does not void the copyright if the work has been previously copyrighted. Care must be taken in copying from government publications to insure that a copyrighted work is not being used without the consent of the copyright proprietor, for the government reprint may not contain the copyright notice.

These provisions obviously present a problem for the federal employee who writes original work, in view of the danger that his work would not be copyrightable if deemed a government publication by the courts. Furthermore, if the writer is a government employee and the work is written within the scope of his employment, the rights in the work may belong to the government under the normal employment-for-hire principle, and the author may be deprived of any benefits that might otherwise be derived from his writings, even if the work would not otherwise constitute a government publication.

Where the government employee does the work on his own time and at his own expense and there is no connection between the material written and the scope of his job, it is clear that he is as much entitled to derive whatever benefits he may from his labor as the person in private employment. Problems arise with respect to material that relates to the job of the government employee but that may be produced on his own time. Unfortunately the statute does not tell us what constitutes a "publication of the United States Government." The clear case is a document printed by the government and prepared by a government employee acting within the scope of his employment. It may be possible for the scholar employed by the government or working on a government project to establish by the terms of his contract that he is to be the copyright proprietor, while granting to the government the right to use and publish the material. Some government agencies have in the past permitted private publication and private copyrighting of job-related work by employees of the agency.

Since 1960 the government has been liable for copyright infringement. Prior thereto it was not possible to successfully sue the government for infringement of copyright.

3. Foreign Works and Works
First Published Abroad

If a foreign work is unpublished, it is entitled to common law copyright protection; the author need not be an American citizen or a resident alien. A foreign work will receive United States copyright protection if it is first published abroad in a country which is a signatory to the Universal Copyright Convention (See Appendix D) or if it is first published abroad and the author is a national of a country which is a signatory if it bears "the symbol © accompanied by the name of the copyright proprietor and the year of first publication placed in such manner and location as to give reasonable notice of claim of copyright." This does not apply to an author who is a United States citizen or a resident alien. Because of the complexities of American copyright law, a book by an American author in a foreign language which is first published abroad is probably in the public domain in the United States. If a book by an American author written in English is first published abroad, it may qualify for *ad interim* copyright. This is a short term of protection until an edition of the work is printed in the United States. Within six months after the first publication outside the United States, a copy of the book (or periodical) must be *received* in the Copyright Office, together with an application on Form A-B Ad Interim and the $4.00 fee. No copyright notice is required on the copy sent to the Copyright Office. Up to 1,500 copies of the work may be imported into the United States, and a proper copyright notice must appear on every copy brought in ("Copyright" or "Copr." or "©," name of the copyright owner, and the year of first publication). An import statement may be obtained from the Copyright Office for presentation to the customs officer when copies are imported into the United States. The ad interim copyright lasts for five years from the first publication abroad. If an American edition is manufactured and published within the five-year-period, the copyright term may be extended to the full term of twenty-eight years. The registration of claim after publication of the American edition must be filed, although it is not essential that this be done within the five-year period.

If the foreign work does not contain a copyright notice, it will probably still be protected under the law of the country of its origin (the United States is one of the few countries which make notice a requirement for copyright), although it will not be protected in the United States. Most foreign countries protect a work for the life of the author plus fifty years. If a book is intended to circulate outside the United States, the foreign copyright must of course be kept in mind.

It is beyond the scope of this work to go into the history of the development of international copyright and the ramifications of the Berne Convention, the Buenos Aires Convention, and presidential proclamations. Suffice it to say in connection with the Buenos Aires Convention, that the phrase "all rights reserved" or the equivalent is a requirement. These words are frequently seen on American works. To the extent that Latin American countries are signatories to the Universal Copyright Convention, such notice is no longer necessary.

4. Translations

The right to make translations is one of the rights granted to the copyright owner by the United States Copyright Act. A translation is also independently copyrightable, even if the original work is in the public domain. In such case anyone would be free to make his own translation of the public domain work, but would not be free to copy the translation. The translation of a public domain work need only bear a copyright notice relating to itself, that is, a notice which contains the year of the first publication of the translation, not the year of the first publication of the work from which it is derived. There is no harm, however, in also including the copyright notice of the underlying work. There is a possibility that if the translation of a copyrighted work does not contain a copyright notice relating to the translation, publication of the translation may divest the copyright in the underlying work.

5. Audio-Visual Material

The scholar who prepares audio-visual material, such as drawings, charts, manuals, motion pictures, filmstrips, slides, tapes, and phonograph records may wish to obtain statutory copyright protection for such works. Before publication, the work will be protected by the common-law copyright. (See Chapter 3.)

Whether or not he can obtain statutory copyright depends upon the kind of audio-visual material. A script for a motion picture or for a sound recording may be registered as an unpublished work. Maps, photographs, and filmstrips may also be so registered. Other unpublished material (such as manuals, outlines, textual summaries, and charts) is not eligible for federal copyright as unpublished work. Phonograph records and tape recordings are not regarded as copies of the material reproduced on them within the meaning of the copyright law; therefore they are not accepted for registration and deposit.

A combination or collection of various material may qualify for registration as a book if the material has been published as a unit with the required copyright notice. The notice requirements (Chapter 6, Section 1) apply as well to audio-visual materials capable of statutory copyright.

The Copyright Office has summarized the registration procedure for audio-visual materials as follows:

Scripts: Form A if published; Form C if unpublished.

Filmstrips or Slides: Form J whether published or unpublished.

Maps: Form F if published; Form I if unpublished and qualified as a "scientific or technical drawing."

Sound Recordings: Phonograph records and tape recordings cannot be registered.

Musical compositions: Form E whether published or unpublished.

Charts and Diagrams: Form G for artistic drawings or sketches; Form I for technical or scientific drawings.

Pictorial Illustrations: Form K for pictorial illustrations reproduced by photolithography or other mechanical process.

Textual Charts: Form A if published; not registerable if unpublished.

Motion Pictures: Form L-M whether published or unpublished.

Copyright registration forms may be obtained by writing to the Copyright Office, Library of Congress, Washington, D.C. 20540.

6. Tapes and Phonograph Records

As has been indicated in previous sections, tapes and phonograph records may not be copyrighted. Protection against unauthorized duplication of sound recordings may possibly be afforded, however, under state law on the basis of an infringement of a common law copyright or on the theory that the unauthorized duplication constitutes unfair competition. The law not only varies from state to state, but is frequently unclear.

Under present law, it is not entirely clear whether a phonograph record is a *publication* of the material on the record. It is recommended that until the law is clarified, any musical composition, play, or speech on a record be registered as an unpublished work before the record is publicly distributed.

On April 19, 1961, a videotape was accepted for registration by the copyright office for the first time. The magnetic videotape recording was Gian Carlo Menotti's opera, *The Consul.*

7. Works of Art

Works of art are copyrightable. Reproductions of works of art are independently copyrightable in the same way that a translation of a work is independently copyrightable. If the work has not been published, it need not contain a copyright notice. There are problems in determining what constitutes publication of a work of art, but it has been said that public exhibition in a gallery or museum where there is no restriction on making copies constitutes a publication. Before reproducing a work of art, therefore, care should be taken to secure the consent of the copyright owner.

The owner of the painting or piece of sculpture may not be the copyright owner. The situation is comparable to that relating to letters, where the recipient may own the letter but the writer owns the right to publish the letter. Similarly, the artist may have reserved the copyright when he sold the painting. More likely, nothing was said about a reservation of copyright in connection with the sale, and it may be unclear who owns the copyright. Even if the painting is obviously in the public domain, as, for example, a painting by Rembrandt, a reproduction of the work appearing in an art publication may be protected by copyright, and while anyone may be free to copy the original, they are not free to copy the copy.

The scholar-artist is well advised to put a copyright notice (See Chapter 6, Section 1) on the work and on all copies. If he sells the work, there should be a written bill of sale, signed by both buyer and seller, stating "Copyright and all rights of reproduction reserved."

8. Illustrations, Maps, Charts, and Tables

The copyrightability of drawings, maps, charts, and tables is discussed in Section 5 of this chapter.

9. Motion Pictures

Motion pictures are subject to copyright. The copyright law provides for two classes of motion pictures. Class L, motion picture photoplays, is for motion pictures that are dramatic in character and tell a connected story, such as theatrical motion pictures, filmed television plays, short subjects having a plot, and animated cartoons. Class M, motion pictures other than photoplays, include newsreels, travelogues, training or promotional films, nature studies, and filmed television programs having no plot. Application in either case is made on Form L-M. All copies of the film that are distributed must bear the proper copyright notice, preferably on the title frame or near it. The year in the copyright notice should be the earliest date when copies of the film are placed on sale, sold, or publicly distributed.

Promptly after publication (See Chapter 3, Section 2), two complete copies of the best edition of the motion picture should be deposited in the Copyright Office together with an application on Form L-M, the registration fee of $4.00, and a description in the form of a synopsis or continuity. Although the copies of the motion picture are subject to retention by the Library of Congress, as is the case with any other work deposited in connection with an application for registration, a contract may be made with the Library of Congress for the return to the applicant of the deposited copies, in view of the fact that motion pictures may represent a substantially greater investment and be more expensive than the usual types of work registered for copyright. For information regarding this contract, the applicant should write to the Exchange and Gift Division, Library of Congress, Washington, D.C. 20540. The copyright office will supply contract forms upon request.

It is possible to register an unpublished motion picture for copyright. (See Chapter 6, Section 2 for the requirements.) If a motion picture is registered as an unpublished work and is subsequently published, the copyright claimant must thereafter deposit an application, registration fee, and two copies of the best edition of the published film bearing the statutory copyright notice. The notice should contain the year of registration as an unpublished work, rather than the year in which the film was first distributed.

10. Contributions to Periodicals and Composite Works

A contribution to a periodical is protected by the general copyright notice of the periodical, because a copyright protects a work and all of its component parts. This is true, however, only if the publisher has acquired all rights in the contribution; otherwise the copyright notice would not be in the proper name. All rights can be transferred to the publisher, subject to an understanding (preferably written) that the copyright and all rights other than magazine publication rights are held in trust by the publisher for the author and will be assigned back to him on request.

If a scholar wishes to retain a separate copyright in his work without any necessity for reassignment, the article or other contribution must contain a separate copyright notice. Unless it does contain a separate copyright notice, a separate copyright registration for the contribution cannot be made. The notice should contain the symbol © or the word "copyright," the author's name, and the year of publication of the periodical containing the contribution (See Chapter 6, Section 1 for a complete discussion of notice requirements).

If the scholar has obtained an independent copyright by having a separate copyright notice on the first page of his contribution, he may register his copyright claim by mailing to the Copyright Office one complete copy of the issue containing the contribution together with an application on Form BB and the registration fee of $4.00.

If the contribution has not been separately copyrighted, it may be possible for the author to secure an assignment of the copyright from the publisher, should there be a need to do so. The courts will sometimes find that the author and the publisher impliedly agreed that the publisher will hold the copyright in trust for the author. If the copyright is assigned and the assignment is recorded in the Copyright Office, any reprint of the contribution *after* the recordation in the Copyright Office may contain the author's name in the copyright notice in place of the name of the prior copyright proprietor. The year in the notice remains unchanged—it must be the year of the first publication. The assignment is recorded by sending the original signed assignment to the Copyright Office with the fee of $3.00, requesting that the assignment be recorded. The original will be photocopied and then returned with a certificate giving the recording data. The assignment should be recorded within three months of the date of execution of the assignment if it was executed in the United States, or within six months if it was executed abroad.

The same procedure may be followed with respect to contributions to encyclopedias, symposium volumes, and other composite works, except that two copies of the complete volume must be submitted with the application and that Form A should be used.

9

How to tell
if a work is protected by copyright

If a work is unpublished, using that word in its conventional sense and not in its technical copyright sense (See Chapter 3, Section 2), it is difficult to determine whether it is in the public domain. If the unpublished work contains a copyright notice, it is apparent that someone is claiming copyright protection. If it contains no notice, it may nevertheless be protected by the common law copyright, which requires no notice. If the work is in the possession of a public library, it would be necessary to investigate how the work came into the library's possession. If it was a gift, were there any restrictions attached? Was there an express or implied consent to publication? Was the common law copyright assigned to the library? Did the grantor have the copyright to assign, or did he own just the physical manuscript? The general subject of copyright in unpublished works is discussed in Chapter 3.

If the work is published and contains a copyright notice (for example, Copyright 1935 by Orlando Bump), it indicates that the work is probably protected by copyright. (*Probably*, because the possibility exists that the work was originally published without a notice, and that the subsequent publication with notice is an improper and ineffective attempt to secure copyright; also, the notice may relate only to the introduction, editorial comment or other new matter, and the rest of the work may be in the public domain.)

If the notice dates back more than fifty-six years, the work is in the public domain (with a possible exception noted below). If it goes back more than twenty-eight years, it is still protected *if* the copyright has been renewed. The original copyright term is twenty-eight years. The copyright may be renewed for an additional twenty-eight years. (See Chapter 6, Section 3.) In almost all foreign countries, copyright protection continues for the life of the author plus a specified number of years (usually fifty) after his death.

Because of the pending revision of the Copyright Law, Congress in 1962 (P. L. 87-668, 87th Congress, Second Session) provided that any renewal term of copyright that was scheduled to expire between September 19, 1962, and December 31, 1965, is automatically continued in force until December 31, 1965. This extension applies only to copyrights whose *second* term (the renewal term) was still in force on September 19, 1962, and would have expired between that date and December 31, 1965.

The Copyright Office will search its records for copyright information on a particular work and report the results, but it will not express an opinion on the legal significance of the facts reported. When requesting a search, as much basic data as possible concerning the work should be given. The Copyright Office will then estimate its fee, based upon a $3.00 per hour rate, and will make the search on receipt of the fee. Information concerning transfers of ownership of a copyright will not be furnished unless specifically requested.

Many of the larger public libraries have available the *Catalog of Copyright Entries* published by the Copyright Office, and the scholar may be able to search that record himself.

The mere fact that the Copyright Office has no record of the work does not mean that it is in the public domain. As pointed out in Chapter 6, Section 2, delay in registration does not invalidate the copyright.

There are attorneys in Washington, D.C. and New York who specialize in copyright searches and who will render an opinion based upon the facts uncovered. In addition to information found by searching the Copyright Office records, these attorneys maintain extensive files of related material and will advise whether any transfers of a copyright have been recorded in the Copyright Office or reported in trade publications dealing with literary and entertainment matters. The scholar's attorney will be able to furnish the names of copyright specialists.

10

Photoduplication
of copyrighted material

In recent years the development of relatively inexpensive methods of photocopying have made the lot of the scholar easier. He is now able to use photocopies of works in the convenience of his own study in situations where it was formerly necessary to visit the library and frequently to spend an inadequate amount of time reviewing the material and copying portions out by hand.

This extraordinary development of chemical and electrostatic methods of photoduplication has presented problems with respect to copyright which have not yet been solved. In May, 1963, a four-day symposium dealing with photocopying and copyright law was held at American University in Washington, D.C. A Committee to Investigate Copyright Problems Affecting Communication in Science and Education, composed of men in education, science, and business, was formed in 1959. It has had several meetings and has circulated reports. There has been considerable discussion of the problem in library journals. In March, 1962, George Fry and Associates made a valuable *Survey of Copyrighted Material Reproduction Practices in Scientific and Technical Fields* for the Office of Science Information Services of the National Science Foundation.

The right to copy is one of the rights reserved to the copyright owner. On the other hand, the researcher, particulary in science and technology, has a great need to obtain copies (frequently multiple copies), and this need has been met by the technological advance in photocopying methods. The amount of literature which must be consulted in the literary and historical fields, and more particularly in the scientific and technical fields, has increased at a phenomenal rate. It has been estimated that our information doubles every ten years. Photocopying is an invaluable tool, and techniques are certain to become easier and less expensive. Computers have already entered the picture. But how can we resolve the copyright problem? Must the library obtain the permission of the copyright owner before it makes a photocopy? Is it violating the copyright owner's exclusive right to make copies if it does not obtain permission? Information must be freely available to those who need it, yet if photocopying becomes a competitor of the publisher to the point where his economic incentive is undermined, the sources of the material being photocopied may dry up.

As indicated in Chapter 7, the doctrine of fair use comes into play with respect to the making of copies of material for purposes of private study. When copying was necessarily done by hand, the problem was not presented in the acute form that it now presents itself. In addition to furnishing photocopies for research and study purposes, libraries and other institutions may also make microfilm or other photocopies to protect rare or perishable works against loss or destruction or against the damage which may be suffered if they are frequently used. As of this writing, there are no reported court cases involving the doctrine of fair use as applied to photocopying by libraries. Under some of the criteria used to determine fair use, it would seem that supplying a photocopy to a scholar for his private use should be regarded as a fair use. On the other hand, it is also clear that supplying a photocopy may interfere with the sale of copies by the publisher. Various factors of availability and relative cost also enter into the picture.

Efforts have been made to formulate a uniform library policy. One result was the "Gentlemen's Agreement" issued in 1937. The Gentlemen's Agreement stated in effect that a single copy of a copyrighted work could be furnished to a scholar for research purposes, provided that the scholar receiving the material is given written notice that he is not exempt from liability to the copyright owner for any infringement resulting from his use of the photocopy and provided that the reproduction is made and furnished without profit to the institution furnishing it.

This agreement, however, was not fully effective. Some of the parties to the agreement are no longer in existence, and many publishers were not signatories; furthermore, the agreement had no force with respect to periodical publishers. Although it had no legal effect, it did reflect what some concerned parties thought of as a fair resolution of the problem. In 1941 the American Library Association adopted a statement of policy that accepted the Gentlemen's Agreement as stating an acceptable view, but incorporated certain additional precautionary rules.

The Library of Congress will normally not furnish a photocopy of copyrighted material without the signed authorization of the copyright owner. University libraries will normally furnish one photocopy of copyrighted material if the user signs a form stating that the copy is solely for scholarly use and is in lieu of manual transcription. The user is also required to assume all responsibility for any violation of the Copyright Act. Some forms also contain an agreement that the user will not reproduce or sell the copy and that he will indemnify the library against any claim of the copyright owner.

With respect to photocopying manuscripts and other unpublished works, a slightly different problem presents itself. It has been said that the doctrine of fair use does not apply to unpublished works. On the other hand, if the common law copyright is viewed as strictly a right of first publication, the furnishing of a photocopy to a scholar for his private use may not be an infringement of such right. Furthermore, it can be argued that the person giving a manuscript to a library or other institution has impliedly authorized the library to make copies available for the use of scholars. The donor may also, however, have attached restrictions to his gift. The reader will recall the distinction between the common law copyright and the ownership right in the physical work itself. It is thus possible that a donor of a manuscript did not own the underlying copyright, which further complicates the situation. It appears likely that if the matter came before a court, the furnishing of a single photocopy for an unpublished work to a scholar for his private use would not constitute an infringement.

Of course, if the work is in the public domain, no copyright problem presents itself. In this connection it must be remembered that, although the underlying work may be in the public domain, the particular version or translation being copied may still be protected by copyright.

The Report of the Register of Copyrights on the General Revision of the U.S. Copyright Law, issued in July, 1961, sums up the matter in this way (page 25 f.):

> The application of the principle of fair use to the making of a photocopy by a library for the use of a person engaged in research is an important question which merits special consideration. This question has not been decided by the courts, and it is uncertain how far a library may go in supplying a photocopy of copyrighted material in its collections. Many libraries and researchers feel that this uncertainty has hampered research and should be resolved to permit the making of photocopies for research purposes to the fullest extent compatible with the interests of copyright owners.
>
> Scholars have always felt free to copy by hand from the works of others for their own private research and study. Aside from the impossibility of controlling copying done in private, the acceptance of this practice may have been based on the inherent limitations of the extent to which copying could be done by hand. But copying has now taken on new dimensions with the development of photocopying devices by which any quantity of material can be reproduced readily and in multiple copies.
>
> Researchers need to have available, for reference and study, the growing mass of published material in their particular fields. This is true especially, though not solely, of material published in scientific, technical, and scholarly journals. Researchers must rely on libraries for much of this material. When a published copy in a library's collection is not available for loan, which is very often the case, the researcher's needs can be met by a photocopy.
>
> On the other hand, the supplying of photocopies of any work to a substantial number of researchers may diminish the copyright owner's market for the work. Publishers of scientific, technical, and scholarly works have pointed out that their market is small; and they have expressed the fear that if many of their potential subscribers or purchasers were furnished with photocopies, they might be forced to discontinue publication.

It is the recommendation of the Register that the Copyright Act should be amended to permit a library whose collections are available to the public without charge to supply a single photocopy of copyrighted material to any applicant under the following conditions:

(a) A single photocopy of one article in any issue of a periodical, or of a reasonable part of any other publication, may be supplied when the applicant states in writing that he needs and will use such material solely for his own research.

(b) A single photocopy of an entire publication may be supplied when the applicant also states in writing and the library is not otherwise informed, that a copy is not available from the publisher.

(c) Where the work bears a copyright notice, the library should be required to affix to the photocopy a warning that the material appears to be copyrighted.

When the scholar wishes to make multiple copies to furnish to research workers or to furnish to members of his class, arrangements should be made with the copyright owner.

11

Noncopyrightable material

1. Ideas, Plans, Theories

An idea or theory may not be copyrighted. Even if the idea is expressed in written form, copyright of the written work does not protect the ideas expressed. It protects only the particular form of expression which the author has chosen to express his ideas. Once a work is published, the idea becomes part of the common stock. For example, an article on an appropriate method of taking notes when doing research for a thesis and a book expressing a completely new theory on the cause of the Civil War may each be copyrighted. If someone else prints or copies the article or book, he has infringed the copyright and is subject to the penalties provided by law. The method of taking notes is not protected, however, and anyone may use the method and may even write an explanation of the method. (Of course, the second explanation, by its very nature, may be very similar to the first, and this is the stuff of which lawsuits are sometimes made.) And anyone may express or write about the novel theory on the cause of the Civil War. To repeat: An idea, plan, theory, scheme, or system cannot be protected by copyright. The social policy reasons for such a principle are obvious.

It should be noted, however, that it is possible to contract with respect to ideas. A person having an idea which he believes to be valuable can offer to disclose the idea if the other party agrees in advance that he will not make any use of the idea unless a mutually agreeable compensation is arrived at. This agreement must be made prior to the disclosure of the idea. Sometimes the courts will imply such a contract by the circumstances of submission. But the only safe procedure is to make no disclosure without an agreement, preferably in writing.

Many companies that frequently receive ideas, such as game manufacturers and advertising agencies, have a form which they require the submitter to sign, indicating that the submitting party is aware that they have many ideas in their own files and that the idea being submitted may be similar to one they have already thought of, and containing various provisions limiting the liability of the receiving party. Sometimes the submitting party has no choice but to sign, but it may nevertheless be possible to make it clear in the submitting letter that the material is being submitted on the condition that it will not be used unless mutually satisfactory compensation is agreed upon. The legal validity of such submission forms may also be open to question.

2. Titles and Names

It is not uncommon to hear someone talk about copyrighting a title. Titles cannot, however, be copyrighted. This does not mean that titles are never protected. If a particular title has become identified in the public mind with a particular work, and if someone else is using that title for another work, the author of the first work may be able to obtain a court order restraining the other party from using that title. The general area of the law which deals with this form of protection is referred to as "unfair competition." The trend of the law is toward greater protection of titles. The protection is obtained, however, not by simply thinking of the title, but by the publication of the work bearing that title, so that the public comes to identify the title with the particular work. Even if the title is a common expression or a generic term, it may be protected if it acquires a "secondary meaning." The names "The Fifth Column" and "Information Please" have been protected by courts. Some kinds of titles are probably incapable of protection, for example, "The History of the Civil War."

Occasionally the court will permit the second use of a title upon the condition that the second user distinguishes his work from the earlier work by an appropriate statement. In a 1908 case, for example, the defendant was permitted to use the title "Webster's Dictionary," but was required to print in large type on the title page of the public domain reprint a statement clearly differentiating it from earlier copyright editions by the plaintiff, whose name had been associated with the famous Webster dictionary from the beginning.

A change in the title of a work does not require (or permit) a new copyright or a new registration in the Copyright Office. It is recommended, however, that in the event of a change of the title of a copyrighted work, a separate signed document be submitted to the Copyright Office giving the old and the new title and the earlier copyright registration data.

3. Obscene and Immoral Works

Copyright registration has been denied on grounds of public policy where the work is obscene or immoral. The difficulty in arriving at adequate definitions and clear standards in this field is amply illustrated by the opinions of the courts in cases involving obscenity. It is presumed that the scholar for whom this book is written will not encounter problems in this area.

4. Works in the Public Domain

All works not protected by common law or statutory copyright are in the public domain. The Copyright Act provides:

No copyright shall exist in the original text of any work which is in the public domain, or in any work which was published in this country or any foreign country prior to July 1, 1909, and has not been copyrighted in the United States.

If a work is in the public domain, it is free for use by anyone. If a scholar edits or annotates a public domain work, he can obtain copyright protection for his contribution—translations, annotations, footnotes, introduction, and other introductory or explanatory material. The law specifically provides that compilations, abridgements, adaptations, arrangements, dramatizations, translations, and other versions of works in the public domain shall be regarded as new works subject to copyright, but the copyright in any such new works does not preclude anyone else from making the same use of the original work. In other words, anyone is free to make an independent adaptation or translation of the public domain work; but they may not copy the copyrighted adaptation, translation, or other version.

5. Government Publications

The Copyright Act specifically excludes from copyright "any publication of the United States Government, or any reprint, in whole or in part thereof." Generally speaking, a government publication is one commissioned or printed at the direction of the United States Government. Questions may arise as to particular works, and it is clear that not every work by a government employee is within this exclusion of the Copyright Act. The subject of government publications is more fully discussed in Chapter 8, Section 2, but it should be noted here that the mere fact of government employment does not mean that every work written by a government employee is a government publication. Certainly the government employee is as free as anyone else to write a novel or a poem during his off-duty hours. In a case of interest to historians, the government was held not to be entitled to certain notes and papers of William Clark made on the Lewis and Clark expedition. A problem which has exercised the courts and which has not yet been finally resolved is whether or not the public speeches made by Admiral Hyman Rickover dealing with education, naval achievements, and other matters are the property of the Admiral or are a government publication and therefore ineligible for copyright.

It should be noted that government use of copyrighted material belonging to someone else does not transform material into a government publication and does not cause any loss of copyright. Even if the scholar consents to government printing of his work, this is probably true. The safest course, however, when the government seeks permission to reprint a work, is to request that the government reprint bear the copyright notice.

Prior to 1960 it was not possible to sue the United States Government for copyright infringement, but now an infringement action may be brought. It is not clear whether a state government is immune from suit for copyright infringement.

12

Patentable inventions

The scholar must either rely upon secrecy to protect his invention or he must patent it. A patent is a grant from the United States Government to an inventor of the exclusive right to make, use, or sell his invention in this country for a limited time. Patents are granted for the invention or discovery of any new and useful process, machine, manufacture, or composition of matter, and improvements thereof; there are also design patents and plant patents. It is not possible to patent a mere idea; the idea must be "reduced to practice," and a practical method of making and using it must be described in a patent application.

Patents are granted for seventeen years, except that a design patent may run for three-and-one-half, seven, or fourteen years, as desired by the patentee. Upon the expiration of a patent, the subject matter it discloses falls into the public domain, and any person may thereafter use the patent without fear of infringement.

The right to a patent will be lost if the invention was described in a "printed publication" in this country or in a foreign country more than one year prior to the date of the application for a patent in the United States. Scholars in the fields of science and engineering should therefore seek the advice of the university attorney or of a private patent law firm before publishing in journal articles or books any materials they may later want to patent. There have been several cases where patent rights have been lost because of premature publication of doctoral dissertations.

A single copy of a dissertation, partly typewritten and partly handwritten, deposited in the library of a state university, is a "printed publication," even though the dissertation is open for inspection only in the university library. A bound copy of a typewritten thesis prepared at a university and placed on the shelves of the library at that institution on a specific date is regarded as a "printed publication" that will constitute a bar against the grant of a patent on the subject matter disclosed in the thesis. A college thesis constitutes "prior art" where it is put on file in the college library, being available to students there and to other libraries having exchange arrangements with the college.

The courts have taken the position that a microfilm normally is not a "printed publication," nor is it "printed" as contemplated in the patent statute. This is a new field, however, and under proper circumstances, the courts might well hold that "printed publication" can be made by microfilming techniques. For example, where a typewritten dissertation is required by the university to be placed on microfilm (See Chapter 1, Section 2), it is evident that the microfilm copy provides the "master" from which an unlimited number of copies of the dissertation can be made and, possibly, sold to members of the public. It has not been decided by the courts that microfilm can under no circumstances be deemed a "printed publication."

The abstract of the dissertation, which is printed separately for public distribution and which is published in *Dissertation Abstracts*, may serve as a bar to the issuance of a patent if it discloses the essential elements of the invention. Patent rights have been lost by a newspaper description of an invention more than a year prior to the filing of the patent application thereon in the Patent Office. A single drawing may, like a written description, constitute publication if it fully discloses the invention.

In order to be copyrighted, a doctoral dissertation must be published; if published, the one-year provision of the patent statute begins on the date of publication. Once the one-year period has lapsed, the right to patent any invention described in the dissertation is lost. Some universities will withhold a dissertation from public circulation if requested to do so by the scholar. Though the following policy of one university is intended primarily to preserve book-publication rights in the dissertation, it would apply equally to patent rights:

> Any dissertation . . . which the author wishes to publish will, upon his request, be withheld from circulation and from microfilming by University Microfilms, Inc. . . . The authorization for such withholding will expire automatically at the end of one calendar year from the date on which the degree is granted unless the time is extended upon petition to the Dean of the Graduate School. The author must promptly notify the Office of University Publications when contract for publication has been secured.

This is a practical arrangement for handling patent rights in dissertations on engineering and science, where the right to a patent may be lost or endangered by premature public disclosure of the contents of the dissertation.

Many persons believe that they can protect their inventions against later inventors merely by mailing to themselves a registered letter describing the invention. This is not true. Priority right against anyone else who makes the same invention independently cannot be sustained except by testimony of someone else who corroborates the inventor's own testimony as to all important facts, such as conception of the invention, diligence in its development, and the success of any tests made.

Witnesses and written records, therefore, are important in establishing priority to an invention. The scholar should prepare a "disclosure," consisting of a written description and drawings made promptly after the invention is conceived; then he should ask two colleagues to read, sign, and date this document as witnesses. He should also keep a carefully dated record of his subsequent work on the invention, and have two friends sign their names as witnesses to the record. Even if a written description or drawing exists, it may still be necessary to prove facts and dates, and the scholar's diligence in completing and testing the invention. To prove any of these things to the satisfaction of the Patent Office or a court, the scholar's own testimony should be supported by one or more other persons who have knowledge of the facts from firsthand observation.

If the scholar thinks he has an invention or a discovery that is patentable, and if he desires to apply for a patent on it, he should seek the services of a patent attorney. (Patent attorneys are generally listed separately in the yellow pages of the telephone directory.) The attorney will examine the invention disclosure and will advise the scholar on the protectable features of his invention; he will also perform a search of the issued patents to determine whether the invention has already been patented. After studying the attorney's report on the search, if the scholar still desires to go ahead with the patent, the attorney will draft a patent application. The application consists of:

(1) Specifications (a description of the invention).
(2) Drawings, where possible, which demonstrate the working of the invention.
(3) Claims, which are the heart of the patent application, consisting of precise definitions of the area of patent protection being sought by the inventor.

The completed application is filed in the Patent Office. Normally it takes about three to five years for a patent to issue in the United States, during which time several "office actions" will be sent to the attorney by the Patent Office. The scholar assists the attorney in preparing "responses" to these office actions. The patent application itself, or any of its claims, can be "abandoned" at any time during the prosecution of the case if the attorney and his client decide that the claims they want are not allowable. When the patent finally issues, the scholar receives the original Letters Patent, an impressive document bearing the official seal of the United States Patent Office. He may also purchase additional printed copies of his patent from the Patent Office.

Copies of issued patents are available for twenty-five cents each from the Commissioner of Patents, Patent Office, U.S. Department of Commerce, Washington, D.C. 20231.

University policies on faculty rights in inventions and discoveries are not uniform. Some institutions observe a strictly hands-off attitude, leaving to the faculty member the responsibility for determining what disposition will be made of the products of his research efforts. Other institutions, maintaining that the university has an interest in all research activity on the campus, have established formalized patent policies. The patent policies and practices of the leading colleges and universities in the United States are summarized in *University Patent Policies and Practices* (Washington, D.C.:

National Academy of Sciences, National Research Council, 1952 and 1955) by Archie M. Palmer. When the university requires its faculty to assign to it the patent rights in inventions and discoveries, there is generally a royalty-sharing arrangement between the inventor and the institution. One large university has the following patent policy in this connection:

> An agreement to assign inventions and patents to the University, except those resulting from permissible consulting activities without use of University facilities, shall be mandatory for all employees, academic and nonacademic. Releases shall be executed, where the equities so indicate, as determined by the University. . . .
>
> The University is averse to seeking protective patents and will not seek such patents unless the discoverer or inventor can demonstrate that the securing of the patent is important to the University.
>
> The University agrees, for and in consideration of said assignment of patent rights, to pay annually to the inventor, his heirs, successors, and assigns, 50 per cent of the royalties and fees received by the University after a deduction of 15 per cent thereof for overhead costs plus a deduction for cost of patenting and protection of patent rights. In the event of any litigation, actual or imminent, or any other action to protect patent rights, the University may withhold distribution and impound royalties until resolution of the matter.

Scholars working for industry are frequently required as a condition of their employment to assign the legal rights in all inventions made by them during the term of their employment to their employers. Some employers pay the inventor an honorarium, part of it at the time the patent application is filed with the Patent Office and the balance when the patent finally issues. The patent is in the name of the inventor, but its commercial exploitation belongs to the employer. If the research that led to the patent was sponsored by the United States Government, the government will have a royalty-free, nonexclusive license throughout the world to use the patent for any governmental purpose.

Some universities and private employers in industry have entered into patent management and development agreements with the Research Corporation, 405 Lexington Avenue, New York, N. Y., a non-profit organization which assists institutions and individuals to obtain patents and market their inventions. The inventor can also obtain guidance about the development and commercial exploitation of his inventions by writing to the National Inventors Council, Department of Commerce, Washington, D.C. 20230, a government-industry liaison agency which seeks to obtain from inventors solutions to technological problems affecting national defense. Finally, the Air Force Systems Command encourages organizations and individuals outside the U.S. Air Force to suggest research and development projects; voluntary unsolicited proposals which contain new ideas, suggestions, and inventive concepts (as well as issued patents) in areas of interest to the Air Force should be submitted by the inventor to Headquarters, Air Force Systems Command, Andrews Air Force Base, Washington, D.C. 20331, Attention: SCMKP-3.

13

Academic freedom and tenure

The basic issues in connection with academic freedom are not legal, but philosophical or social. We must determine the proper function of the university in our society, and we must agree upon the best way to encourage the university to fulfill that function. Academic freedom exists for the good of society and not for the benefit of a particular scholar. It is society that will benefit by permitting the spirit of inquiry to flourish in the university community.

There is no constitutional guarantee of academic freedom; this concept is one of our more recent liberties. In Greek and Roman times, slaves were frequently the teachers. Academic freedom has been variously defined, but it is basically the right of the scholar to speak, write, and carry on research without interference by the university or the government. Generally it is the freedom of the scholar in his classroom, library, or laboratory, but conduct of the scholar outside of the university is relevant, and the scholar should have the same right to speak freely outside of the classroom as any other citizen. It has been well said that thought and speech are not extracurricular activities for the scholar, as is the case for most persons; they are his occupation. At different times in our history, questions of academic freedom have involved different subjects, for example, the abolition of slavery, Darwin's theory of evolution, bimetallism, the propriety of loyalty oaths.

It is perhaps inevitable that there be conflict between the regents or trustees of a university, who usually represent the dominant groups in the community, and scholars whose independence and research may lead to "troublesome" ideas and may be influential agents for change.

The right of the scholar to teach, write, and carry on research is not necessarily a legal right. Other than the general constitutional provisions concerning freedom of speech and expression, there is no law or constitutional provision which says that the scholar must have freedom to pursue the truth without regard to where the path may lead. Furthermore, the scholar is subject to the same limitations as all other citizens with respect to such limitations on the right to speak as libel, laws relating to the incitement of crime, and the like.

Academic freedom should not be confused with tenure, although tenure may be a necessary condition to the full blossoming of academic freedom. (But even where tenure exists, there are many pressures and penalties other than dismissal or its threat that may restrict academic freedom.)

Tenure is the concept that faculty members who have served a proper period of apprenticeship have the right to continue in their positions, subject to removal only for adequate cause. The concept is not unique in the academic profession, although it is frequently discussed as if it were. A comparable notion may be found in the civil service, in religious institutions, and sometimes among the trustees of educational institutions. Under the United States Constitution federal judges hold their position "for life during good behavior."

There is a wide range of tenure systems in American education with considerable variation in detail. The best treatment of the subject is *Tenure in American Higher Education: Plans, Practices, and the Law* by Clark Byse and Louis Joughin (Ithaca, Cornell U.P., 1959). This chapter draws heavily on that work. There is also a considerable amount of material relating both to tenure and academic freedom to be found from time to time in the *Bulletin of the American Association of University Professors*. The Byse and Joughin book contains in an appendix the 1940 Statement of Principles on Academic Freedom and Tenure adopted by the American Association of University Professors and the Association of American Colleges.

The legal remedy for a violation of tenure in a *state* institution would be to seek a court order directing the governing board to reinstate the dismissed faculty member on the basis that the tenure plan adopted by the board has the force of law and that a dismissal contrary to the law is outside of the board's authority. The court would be asked to enforce the law by ordering reinstatement. In a *private* institution the relationship would be contractual, which presents important limitations on the rights of the dismissed scholar. At best he may be entitled to a judgment for money. Normally the remedy for a breach of contract is a suit for damages. The measure of damages in a suit by an employee is usually what he would have earned had the contract not been breached, less the amount he has earned or could reasonably have earned elsewhere. Under certain circumstances there is a remedy of specific performance, that is, the court orders that the contract be performed, but this remedy is usually not available where the contract involves personal services.

There are considerable drawbacks to any attempt to legally enforce tenure rights. The procedure may be expensive and take a long time, and the scholar may be reluctant to have a public airing of the matter in controversy. So legal enforceability is probably not the most important element in connection with tenure. It is probably more important that there be a set of clear rules relating to tenure and obedience to those rules by a responsible faculty and administration. In the last analysis, however, when there is no other recourse, it is to the court that the scholar must turn. Furthermore, the existence of the legal remedy may be sufficient to curb the otherwise uncontrolled discretion of the administration or governing board. Also, a legal right on the part of a faculty member may better enable an administrator to resist public pressures. The great significance of the law lies in the widespread obedience to law and not in the rare violations.

To resort to court action, there must be a legally enforceable obligation by the institution to the scholar, but there are barriers to the creation of such an obligation. For example, the charters of some institutions contain provisions giving the trustees the power to remove faculty members at will. It has been held by some courts that this kind of provision precludes the making of a binding contract between the university and the professor; other courts have interpreted this kind of provision as not preventing the making of a contract which is for a limited period. Some tenure plans contain specific statements to the effect that they do not create any binding contractual obligation. Other plans contain ambiguities and poor draftmanship that lead to unenforceability. These are matters that are determined normally by state courts, and it is not unusual in the law to have two different lines of decisions, or minority and majority views—that is, a group of cases taking one view and a group of cases in other jurisdictions taking a different view. (For a comprehensive discussion of the subject of court review of *student* expulsions, see the lengthy discussion in 72 *Yale Law Review* 1362, "Private Government on the Campus—Judicial Review of University Expulsions.")

There have been successful court cases, however, such as that of the professors involved in the loyalty-oath controversy at the University of California and the case of Professor Frank Richardson at the University of Nevada in 1954.

The court has the great virtue of furnishing an independent forum, although it must give due weight to the opinion of the faculty member's colleagues and the administration. The courts have not always distinguished themselves, and the Bertrand Russell case, in which it was held that the Board of Higher Education of New York City had no right to appoint the distinguished philosopher as professor of philosophy at the College of the City of New York is a sorry example. In any particular case, the various relevant documents must be examined: the charter of the institution, the rules or regulations of the institution relating to tenure, the letter of appointment of the faculty member involved, and so on.

If a faculty member is discharged, it is fundamental that the discharge should take place consistent with principles of due process. The faculty member should have the right to be present at a hearing, to be represented by counsel of his own choosing, to cross-examine witnesses, to present and summon witnesses, to an available full record, to meaningful appeal procedures, to prompt adjudication, and to a separation of the prosecuting and the judicial functions.

Among the recommendations made by Byse and Joughin are the following:

> Because of the importance of enforcement by an independent judiciary, those institutions with charters and plans containing provisions which hinder legal enforcement should adopt corrective

amendments eliminating or clarifying authorizations to discharge at will, disclaimer clauses, finality provisions, confusing ambiguities, and vague termination criteria which only remotely bear upon a faculty member's fitness to teach, to engage in research, or to associate with students. . . .

The creative judge, recognizing the vital importance of academic freedom in our society and its customary acknowledgment in long-established usage, should feel free to hold that in the absence of a specific disclaimer or finality clause, the faculty member of long service has acquired a *status* and that an incident of this status is protection from discharge except for good cause and after proceedings which comply with the principles of academic due process. The remedy for infringement of tenure should include an order of reinstatement.

If the universities are to fulfill their function, and if the scholar is to be free from restraints and pressures that inhibit freedom of thought, the scholar needs not only the protection of the constitutional amendments which are given to every citizen, but also needs protection from dismissal from his position without cause. Tenure is the principal means of protection against unjustified dismissals.

14

Some miscellaneous legal problems

1. Defamation: Libel and Slander

One of the areas of the law with which the scholar may be concerned is the law of defamation. Defamation, generally, is a violation of a person's right not to have his reputation injured by false statements. When the regard in which a person is held by others is adversely affected by the publication of a false statement, the injured party may bring an action for defamation. The defamatory matter must have been "published," that is, communicated to a third person or persons, in order for it to constitute grounds for suit. (Note that "publication" in the law of defamation has a different meaning than it does in copyright law.) Without such communication no actionable defamation exists. It may be sufficient if the matter has been communicated to only one person other than the person defamed.

Defamation is divided into two broad classes, libel and slander. Speaking generally, the wrong is called libel if the defamatory publication is embodied in a permanent form, such as a writing or a photograph; if the wrong is an oral communication, it is slander. The courts have had to wrestle with such problems as whether defamation on a radio program or a live television show or by a phonograph record are libel or slander. The distinction is important, because the classification into which the conduct falls will affect various aspects of the legal action. Generally, the victim of a libel may sue without any proof of actually having been damaged, whereas only certain kinds of slander may be the basis of suit without proof of actual damages—for example, a statement that charges the commission of a crime or that tends to injure a party in his business, trade or profession, or that imputes to him certain loathsome diseases; this kind of statement is called libel or slander *per se*.

The defamatory statement need not be defamatory in the words used. Sometimes a statement is defamatory only with respect to facts that may be unstated in the defamatory statement itself. For example, a charge that a woman is the mother of three children may be defamatory if she is not and never has been married; a charge that a man is associated with John Doe in all of his business ventures may be defamatory if John Doe is a known criminal.

In most states, truth is a complete defense to an action for defamation. If the defamatory statement is true, the injured party cannot recover, regardless of the extent of his injuries and regardless of the motive of the defamer in making the statements; but the burden is on the defendant to prove that the statements were true.

In certain situations, for reasons of public policy, the defamatory statement will be privileged, that is, the maker will not be subject to liability. Some statements are absolutely privileged, which means that the defendant's purpose or motive is irrelevant. Some statements are conditionally or qualifiedly privileged, which means that if the defendant acted out of malice or without any grounds for believing the truth of his statement, the privilege is defeated. For example, statements made in Congress or other legislative bodies are absolutely privileged and do not give rise to any basis for a suit even though they might be extremely adverse and totally false. The same thing is true of statements made in the course of a judicial proceeding. The public policy underlying this defense is not difficult to see. We wish to encourage the fullest and freest speech in legislative proceedings and in judicial proceedings.

A false and defamatory statement may be the subject of a "qualified" privilege when the relationship between the person making the statement and the person to whom the statement is made is such that it is reasonable and proper that the information should be given. A statement by a father to his daughter that her fiancé is a bum would be subject to a qualified privilege. "Fair comment," or criticism of matters of public concern, is qualifiedly privileged. A common example of fair comment is the criticism that may be made by critics or reviewers of a book or play or the criticism of a public figure by newspaper columnists. A classic case involved the newspaper review of a vaudeville act which said:

> Effie is an old jade of fifty summers, Jessie a frisky filly of forty, and Addie, the flower of the family, a capering monstrosity of thirty-five. Their long skinny arms, equipped with talons at the extremities, swing mechanically, and anon waved frantically at the suffering audience. The mouths of their rancid features opened like caverns, and sounds like the wailings of damned souls issued therefrom. [Held fair comment.]

Many states have laws relating to the retraction of defamatory statements. In California, for example, a retraction by a newspaper will prevent the recovery of general damages, and the plaintiff will be able to recover only the actual out-of-pocket damages which he can prove. Obviously this is an extremely difficult burden of proof.

The law of defamation varies from state to state in important respects, and the law of the particular jurisdiction must be examined in any particular case. This is also true of the right of privacy discussed in the next section.

2. Right of Privacy

One of the most famous law-review articles in legal history was that written by Louis D. Brandeis (later Mr. Justice Brandeis) and his former law partner Samuel D. Warren and published in the *Harvard Law Review* in 1890. This article drew together decisions in which the courts had granted relief on various legal theories and urged that the cases cited were really based upon a principle which they called the "right to privacy," which, they argued, was entitled to separate recognition. This right has been the subject of very extensive examination by legal scholars, and there are many discussions of the right in legal periodicals. It has also been called "the right to be let alone."

In a penetrating law review article, William L. Prosser, former Dean of the University of California School of Law, came to the conclusion that the right of privacy was really a complex of four different kinds of invasion of four different interests of the individual harmed. These four wrongs he described as follows:

(1) Intrusion upon the plaintiff's seclusion or solitude, or into his private affairs.
(2) Public disclosure of embarrassing private facts about the plaintiff.
(3) Publicity which places the plaintiff in a false light in the public eye.
(4) Appropriation, for the defendant's advantage, of the plaintiff's name or likeness.

The following are two of the best-known cases dealing with the right of privacy. William James Sidis, the son of a Harvard professor of psychology, an infant prodigy, and a graduate of Harvard at the age of sixteen, filed suit against the *New Yorker* magazine. Sidis had lost his great interest in mathematics and was leading an obscure life as a bookkeeper, collecting streetcar transfers. The *New Yorker* published a "profile" revealing his background and his then current activities. Sidis lost his case.

An ex-prostitute, who had been tried for murder and acquitted, settled down to a respectable life in California among people who were unaware of her earlier career. Seven years later a motion picture called "The Red Kimono" was made, relating the story of her past and revealing the story to her friends. The California court held that this was an invasion of her right of privacy.

If the scholar's work is based upon interviews or questionnaires, care must be taken in reporting the results of such research in order that the right of privacy of the scholar's informants is not invaded. An informant should not be identified by name unless his consent is obtained. A sound practice is to send the informant a copy of the statement which the scholar intends to attribute to him, asking him to make any corrections and to sign and return a copy of the letter. In any treatment of living persons, the right of privacy must be considered. Generally, public figures are held to have waived their right of privacy, at least insofar as their public activities are concerned.

3. Tort Liability of Teachers

The cases and commentaries dealing with the liability of a teacher for intentionally or negligently inflicted injury to a pupil have usually concerned the right of a teacher to enforce discipline. Although the enforcement of discipline does not seem to have diminished as a problem, the imposition of corporal punishment seems largely to have ceased, at least at the college level. Because this work is intended for use by scholars at the college and university level, the general subject of a teacher's tort liability will not be discussed. Again, this is a matter that is controlled by the law of the particular state in which the conduct occurs.

Appendix A

Copyright law
of the United States of America

**United States Code
Title 17—Copyrights[1]**

Chapter 1—Registration of copyrights

§ 1. Exclusive rights as to copyrighted works.
§ 2. Rights of author or proprietor of unpublished work.
§ 3. Protection of component parts of work copyrighted; composite works or periodicals.
§ 4. All writings of author included.
§ 5. Classification of works for registration.
§ 6. Registration of prints and labels.
§ 7. Copyright on compilations of works in public domain or of copyrighted works; subsisting copyrights not affected.

---

[1] Act of July 30, 1947 (61 Stat. 652). The enacting clause provides that Title 17 of the United States Code entitled "Copyrights" is codified and enacted into positive law and may be cited as "Title 17, U.S.C., § —".

§ 8. Copyright not to subsist in works in public domain, or published prior to July 1, 1909, and not already copyrighted, or government publications; publication by government of copyrighted material.

§ 9. Authors or proprietors, entitled; aliens.

§ 10. Publication of work with notice.

§ 11. Registration of claim and issuance of certificate.

§ 12. Works not reproduced for sale.

§ 13. Deposit of copies after publication; action or proceeding for infringement.

§ 14. Same; failure to deposit; demand; penalty.

§ 15. Same; postmaster's receipt; transmission by mail without cost.

§ 16. Mechanical work to be done in United States.

§ 17. Affidavit to accompany copies.

§ 18. Making false affidavit.

§ 19. Notice; form.

§ 20. Same; place of application of; one notice in each volume or number of newspaper or periodical.

§ 21. Same; effect of accidental omission from copy or copies.

§ 22. Ad interim protection of book or periodical published abroad.

§ 23. Same; extension to full term.

§ 24. Duration; renewal and extension.

§ 25. Renewal of copyrights registered in Patent Office under repealed law.

§ 26. Terms defined.

§ 27. Copyright distinct from property in object copyrighted; effect of sale of object and of assignment of copyright.

§ 28. Assignments and bequests.

§ 29. Same; executed in foreign country; acknowledgment and certificate.

§ 30. Same; record.

§ 31. Same; certificate of record.

§ 32. Same; use of name of assignee in notice.

§ 1. **Exclusive Rights as to Copyrighted Works.**—Any person entitled thereto, upon complying with the provisions of this title, shall have the exclusive right:

(a) To print, reprint, publish, copy, and vend the copyrighted work;

(b) To translate the copyrighted work into other languages or dialects, or make any other version therof, if it be a literary work; to dramatize it if it be a nondramatic work; to convert it into a novel or other nondramatic work if it be a drama; to arrange or adapt it if it be a musical work; to complete, execute, and finish it if it be a model or design for a work of art;

(c) To deliver, authorize the delivery of, read, or present the copyrighted work in public for profit if it be a lecture, sermon, address, or similar production, or other nondramatic literary work; to make or procure the making of any transcription or record thereof by or from which, in whole or in part, it may in any manner or by any method be exhibited, delivered, presented, produced, or reproduced; and to play or perform it in public for profit, and to exhibit, represent, produce, or reproduce it in any manner or by any method whatsoever. The damages for the infringement by broadcast of any work referred to in this subsection shall not exceed the sum of $100 where the infringing broadcaster shows that he was not aware that he was infringing and that such infringement could not have been reasonably foreseen; and

(d) To perform or represent the copyrighted work publicly if it be a drama or, if it be a dramatic work and not reproduced in copies for sale, to vend any manuscript or any record whatsoever thereof; to make or to procure the making of any transcription or record thereof by or from which, in whole or in part, it may in any manner or by any method be exhibited, performed, represented, produced, or reproduced; and to exhibit, perform, represent, produce, or reproduce it in any manner or by any method whatsoever; and

(e) To perform the copyrighted work publicly for profit if it be a musical composition; and for the purpose of public performance for profit, and for the purposes set forth in subsection (a) hereof, to make any arrangement or setting of it or of the melody of it in any system of notation or any form of record in which the thought of an author may be recorded and from which it may be read or reproduced: *Provided,* That the provisions of this title, so far as they secure copyright controlling the parts of instruments serving to reproduce mechanically the musical work, shall include only compositions published and copyrighted after July 1, 1909, and shall not include the works of a foreign author or composer unless the foreign state or nation of which such author or composer is a citizen or subject grants, either by treaty, convention, agreement, or law, to citizens of the United States similar rights. And as a condition of extending the copyright control to such mechanical reproductions, that whenever the owner of a musical copyright has used or permitted or knowingly acquiesced in the use of the copyrighted work upon the parts of instruments serving to reproduce mechanically the musical work, any other person may make similar use of the copyrighted work upon the payment to the copyright proprietor of a royalty of 2 cents on each such part manufactured, to be paid by the manufacturer thereof; and the copyright proprietor may require, and if so the manufacturer shall furnish, a report under oath on the 20th day of each month on the number of parts of instruments manufactured during the previous month serving to reproduce mechanically said musical work, and royalties shall be due on the parts manufactured during any month upon the 20th of the next succeeding month. The payment of the royalty provided for by this section shall free the articles or devices for which such royalty has been paid from further contribution to the copyright except in case of public performance for profit. It shall be the duty of the copyright owner, if he uses the musical composition himself for the manufacture of parts of instruments serving to reproduce mechanically the musical work, or licenses others to do so, to file notice thereof, accompanied by a recording fee, in the copyright office, and any failure to file such notice shall be a complete defense to any suit, action, or proceeding for any infringement of such copyright.

In case of failure of such manufacturer to pay to the copyright proprietor within thirty days after demand in writing the full sum of royalties due at said rate at the date of such demand, the court may award taxable costs to the plaintiff and a reasonable counsel fee, and the court may, in its discretion, enter judgment therein for any sum in addition over the amount found to be due as royalty in accordance with the terms of this title, not exceeding three times such amount.

The reproduction or rendition of a musical composition by or upon coin-operated machines shall not be deemed a public performance for profit unless a fee is charged for admission to the place where such reproduction or rendition occurs.

§ 2. **Rights of Author or Proprietor of Unpublished Work.**—Nothing in this title shall be construed to annul or limit the right of the author or proprietor of an unpublished work, at common law or in equity, to prevent the copying, publication, or use of such unpublished work without his consent, and to obtain damages therefor.

§ 3. **Protection of Component Parts of Work Copyrighted; Composite Works or Periodicals.**—The copyright provided by this title shall protect all the copyrightable component parts of the work copyrighted, and all matter therein in which copyright is already subsisting, but without extending the duration or scope of such copyright. The copyright upon composite works or periodicals shall give to the proprietor thereof all the rights in respect thereto which he would have if each part were individually copyrighted under this title.

§ 4. **All Writings of Author Included.**—The works for which copyright may be secured under this title shall include all the writings of an author.

§ 5. **Classification of Works for Registration.**—The application for registration shall specify to which of the following classes the work in which copyright is claimed belongs:

(a) Books, including composite and cyclopedic works, directories, gazetteers, and other compilations.

(b) Periodicals, including newspapers.

(c) Lectures, sermons, addresses (prepared for oral delivery).

(d) Dramatic or dramatico-musical compositions.

(e) Musical compositions.

(f) Maps.

(g) Works of art; models or designs for works of art.

(h) Reproductions of a work of art.

(i) Drawings or plastic works of a scientific or technical character.

(j) Photographs.

(k) Prints and pictorial illustrations, including prints or labels used for articles of merchandise.

(1) Motion-picture photoplays.

(m) Motion pictures other than photoplays.

The above specifications shall not be held to limit the subject-matter of copyright as defined in section 4 of this title, nor shall any error in classification invalidate or impair the copyright protection secured under this title.

§ 6. **Registration of Prints and Labels.**—Commencing July 1, 1940, the Register of Copyrights is charged with the registration of claims to copyright properly presented, in all prints and labels published in connection with the sale or advertisement of articles of merchandise, including all claims to copyright in prints and labels pending in the Patent Office and uncleared at the close of business June 30, 1940. There shall be paid for registering a claim of copyright in any such print or label not a trade-mark $6, which sum shall cover the expense of furnishing a certificate of such registration, under the seal of the Copyright Office, to the claimant of copyright.

§ 7. **Copyright on Compilations of Works in Pubic Domain or of Copyrighted Works; Subsisting Copyrights Not Affected.**—Compilations or abridgments, adaptations, arrangements, dramatizations, translations, or other versions of works in the public domain or of copyrighted works when produced with the consent of the proprietor of the copyright in such works, or works republished with new matter, shall be regarded as new works subject to copyright under the provisions of this title; but the publication of any such new works shall not affect the force or validity of any subsisting copyright upon the matter employed or any part thereof, or be construed to imply an exclusive right to such use of the original works, or to secure or extend copyright in such original works.

§ 8. **Copyright Not to Subsist in Works in Public Domain, or Published Prior to July 1, 1909, and Not Already Copyrighted, or Government Publications; Publication by Government of Copyrighted Material.**—No copyright shall subsist in the original text of any work which is in the public domain, or in any work which was published in this country or any foreign country prior to July 1, 1909, and has not been already copyrighted in the United States, or in any publication of the United States Government, or any reprint, in whole or in part, thereof: *Provided,* That copyright may be secured by the Postmaster General on behalf of the United States in the whole or any part of the publications authorized by section 1 of the Act of January 27, 1938 (39 U.S.C. 371).

The publication or republication by the government, either separately or in a public document, of any material in which copyright is subsisting shall not be taken to cause any abridgment or annulment of the copyright or to authorize any use or appropriation of such copyright material without the consent of the copyright proprietor.

§ 9. **Authors or Proprietors, Entitled: Aliens.**—The author or proprietor of any work made the subject of copyright by this title, or his executors, administrators, or assigns, shall have copyright for such work under the conditions and for the terms specified in this title: *Provided, however,* That the copyright secured by this title shall extend to the work of an author or proprietor who is a citizen or subject of a foreign state or nation only under the conditions described in subsections (a), (b), or (c) below:

(a) When an alien author or proprietor shall be domiciled within the United States at the time of the first publication of his work; or

(b) When the foreign state or nation of which such author or pro- prietor is a citizen or subject grants, either by treaty, convention, agree- ment, or law, to citizens of the United States the benefit of copyright on substantially the same basis as to its own citizens, or copyright pro- tection substantially equal to the protection secured to such foreign author under this title or by treaty; or when such foreign state or nation is a party to an international agreement which provides for reciprocity in the granting of copyright, by the terms of which agreement the United States may, at its pleasure, become a party thereto.

The existence of the reciprocal conditions aforesaid shall be deter- mined by the President of the United States, by proclamation made from time to time, as the purposes of this title may require: *Provided,* That whenever the President shall find that the authors, copyright owners, or proprietors of works first produced or published abroad and subject to copyright or to renewal of copyright under the laws of the United States, including works subject to ad interim copyright, are or may have been temporarily unable to comply with the conditions and formalities prescribed with respect to such works by the copyright laws of the United States, because of the disruption or suspension of facilities essential for such compliance, he may by proclamation grant such ex- tension of time as he may deem appropriate for the fulfillment of such conditions or formalities by authors, copyright owners, or proprietors who are citizens of the United States or who are nationals of countries which accord substantially equal treatment in this respect to authors, copyright owners, or proprietors who are citizens of the United States: *Provided further,* That no liability shall attach under this title for lawful uses made or acts done prior to the effective date of such proclamation in connection with such works, or in respect to the continuance for one year subsequent to such date of any business undertaking or enterprise law- fully undertaken prior to such date involving expenditure or contractual obligation in connection with the exploitation, production, reproduction, circulation, or performance of any such work.

The President may at any time terminate any proclamation authorized herein or any part thereof or suspend or extend its operation for such period or periods of time as in his judgment the interests of the United States may require.

(c) When the Universal Copyright Convention, signed at Geneva on September 6, 1952, shall be in force[2] between the United States of America and the foreign state or nation of which such author is a citizen or subject, or in which the work was first published. Any work to which copyright is extended pursuant to this subsection shall be exempt from the following provisions of this title: (1) The requirement in section 1 (e) that a foreign state or nation must grant to United States citizens mechanical reproduction rights similar to those specified therein; (2) the obligatory deposit requirements of the first sentence of section 13; (3) the provisions of sections 14, 16, 17, and 18; (4) the import prohibitions of section 107, to the extent that they are related to the manufacturing requirements of section 16; and (5) the requirements of sections 19 and 20: *Provided, however,* That such exemptions shall apply only if from the time of first publication all the copies of the work published with the authority of the author or other copyright proprietor shall bear the symbol © accompanied by the name of the copyright proprietor and the year of first publication placed in such manner and location as to give reasonable notice of claim of copyright.

Upon the coming into force of the Universal Copyright Convention in a foreign state or nations as hereinbefore provided, every book or periodical of a citizen or subject thereof in which ad interim copyright was subsisting on the effective date of said coming into force shall have copyright for twenty-eight years from the date of first publication abroad without the necessity of complying with the further formalities specified in section 23 of this title.

The provisions of this subsection shall not be extended to works of an author who is a citizen of, or domiciled in the United States of America regardless of place of first publication, or to works first published in the United States.

§ 10. **Publication of Work with Notice.**—Any person entitled thereto by this title may secure copyright for his work by publication thereof with the notice of copyright required by this title; and such notice shall be affixed to each copy thereof published or offered for sale in the United States by authority of the copyright proprietor, except in the case of books seeking ad interim protection under section 22 of this title.

§ 11. **Registration of Claim and Issuance of Certificate.**—Such person may obtain registration of his claim to copyright by complying with the provisions of this title, including the deposit of copies, and upon such compliance the Register of Copyrights shall issue to him the certificates provided for in section 209 of this title.

§ 12. **Works Not Reproduced for Sale.**—Copyright may also be had of the works of an author, of which copies are not reproduced for sale, by the deposit, with claim of copyright, of one complete copy of such work if it be a lecture or similar production or a dramatic, musical, or dramatico-musical composition; of a title and description, with one

---

[2] The Universal Copyright Convention came into force on September 16, 1955.

print taken from each scene or act, if the work be a motion-picture photoplay; of a photographic print, if the work be a photograph; of a title and description, with not less than two prints taken from different sections of a complete motion picture, if the work be a motion picture other than a photoplay; or of a photograph or other identifying reproduction therof, if it be a work of art or a plastic work or drawing. But the privilege of registration of copyright secured hereunder shall not exempt the copyright proprietor from the deposit of copies, under sections 13 and 14 of this title, where the work is later reproduced in copies for sale.

§ 13. **Deposit of Copies After Publication; Action or Proceeding for Infringement.**—After copyright has been secured by publication of the work with the notice of copyright as provided in section 10 of this title, there shall be promptly deposited in the Copyright Office or in the mail addressed to the Register of Copyrights, Washington, District of Columbia, two complete copies of the best edition thereof then published, or if the work is by an author who is a citizen or subject of a foreign state or nation and has been published in a foreign country, one complete copy of the best edition then published in such foreign country, which copies or copy, if the work be a book or periodical, shall have been produced in accordance with the manufacturing provisions specified in section 16 of this title; or if such work be a contribution to a periodical, for which contribution special registration is requested, one copy of the issue or issues containing such contribution; or if the work belongs to a class specified in subsections (g), (h), (i), or (k) of section 5 of this title, and if the Register of Copyrights determines that it is impracticable to deposit copies because of their size, weight, fragility, or monetary value, he may permit the deposit of photographs or other identifying reproductions in lieu of copies of the work as published under such rules and regulations as he may prescribe with the approval of the Librarian of Congress; or if the work is not reproduced in copies for sale there shall be deposited the copy, print, photograph, or other identifying reproduction provided by section 12 of this title, such copies or copy, print, photograph, or other reproduction to be accompanied in each case by a claim of copyright. No action or proceeding shall be maintained for infringement of copyright in any work until the provisions of this title with respect to the deposit of copies and registration of such work shall have been complied with.

§ 14. **Same; Failure to Deposit; Demand; Penalty.**—Should the copies called for by section 13 of this title not be promptly deposited as provided in this title, the Register of Copyrights may at any time after the publication of the work, upon actual notice, require the proprietor of the copyright to deposit them, and after the said demand shall have been made, in default of the deposit of copies of the work within three months from any part of the United States, except an outlying territorial possession of the United States, or within six months from any outlying territorial possession of the United States, or from any foreign country, the proprietor of the copyright shall be liable to a fine of $100 and to pay to the Library of Congress twice the amount of the retail price of the best edition of the work, and the copyright shall become void.

§ 15. **Same; Postmaster's Receipt; Transmission by Mail Without Cost.**—The postmaster to whom are delivered the articles deposited as provided in sections 12 and 13 of this title shall, if requested, give a receipt therefor and shall mail them to their destination without cost to the copyright claimant.

§ 16. **Mechanical Work To Be Done in United States.**—Of the printed book or periodical specified in section 5, subsections (a) and (b), of this title, except the original text of a book or periodical of foreign origin in a language or languages other than English, the text of all copies accorded protection under this title, except as below provided, shall be printed from type set within the limits of the United States, either by hand or by the aid of any kind of typesetting machine, or from plates made within the limits of the United States from type set therein, or, if the text be produced by lithographic process, or photoengraving process, then by a process wholly performed within the limits of the United States, and the printing of the text and binding of the said book shall be performed within the limits of the United States; which requirements shall extend also to the illustrations within a book consisting of printed text and illustrations produced by lithographic process, or photoengraving process, and also to separate lithographs or photoengravings, except where in either case the subjects represented are located in a foreign country and illustrate a scientific work or reproduce a work of art: *Provided, however,* That said requirements shall not apply to works in raised characters for the use of the blind, or to books or periodicals of foreign origin in a language or languages other than English, or to works printed or produced in the United States by any other process than those above specified in this section, or to copies of books or periodicals, first published abroad in the English language, imported into the United States within five years after first publication in a foreign state or nation up to the number of fifteen hundred copies of each such book or periodical if said copies shall contain notice of copyright in accordance with sections 10, 19, and 20 of this title and if ad interim copyright in said work shall have been obtained pursuant to section 22 of this title prior to the importation into the United States of any copy except those permitted by the provisions of section 107 of this title: *Provided further,* That the provisions of this section shall not affect the right of importation under the provisions of section 107 of this title.

§ 17. **Affidavit To Accompany Copies.**—In the case of the book the copies so deposited shall be accompanied by an affidavit under the official seal of any officer authorized to administer oaths within the United States, duly made by the person claiming copyright or by his duly authorized agent or representative residing in the United States, or by the printer who has printed the book, setting forth that the copies deposited have been printed from type set within the limits of the United States or from plates made within the limits of the United States from type set therein; or, if the text be produced by lithographic process, or photoengraving process, that such process was wholly performed within the limits of the United States and that the printing of the text and binding of the said book have also been performed within the limits of the United States. Such affidavit shall state also the place where and the establishment or establishments in which such type was set or plates were made or lithographic process, or photoengraving process or printing and binding were performed and the date of the completion of the printing of the book or the date of publication.

§ 18. **Making False Affidavit.**—Any person who, for the purpose of obtaining registration of a claim to copyright, shall knowingly make a false affidavit as to his having complied with the above conditions shall be deemed guilty of a misdemeanor, and upon conviction thereof shall be punished by a fine of not more than $1,000, and all of his rights and privileges under said copyright shall thereafter be forfeited.

§ 19. **Notice; Form.**—The notice of copyright required by section 10 of this title shall consist of the word "Copyright," the abbreviation "Copr.," or the symbol ©, accompanied by the name of the copyright proprietor, and if the work be a printed literary, musical, or dramatic work, the notice shall include also the year in which the copyright was secured by publication. In the case, however, of copies of works specified in subsections (f) to (k), inclusive, of section 5 of this title, the notice may consist of the letter C enclosed within a circle, thus ©, accompanied by the initials, monogram, mark, or symbol of the copyright proprietor: *Provided,* That on some accessible portion of such copies or of the margin, back, permanent base, or pedestal, or of the substance on which such copies shall be mounted, his name shall appear. But in the case of works in which copyright was subsisting on July 1, 1909, the notice of copyright may be either in one of the forms prescribed herein or may consist of the following words: "Entered according to Act of Congress, in the year   , by A. B., in the office of the Librarian of Congress, at Washington, D.C.," or, at his option, the word "Copyright," together with the year the copyright was entered and the name of the party by whom it was taken out; thus, "Copyright, 19—, by A. B."

§ 20. **Same; Place of Application of; One Notice in Each Volume or Number of Newspaper or Periodical.**—The notice of copyright shall be applied, in the case of a book or other printed publication, upon its title page or the page immediately following, or if a periodical either upon the title page or upon the first page of text of each separate number or under the title heading, or if a musical work either upon its title page or the first page of music. One notice of copyright in each volume or in each number of a newspaper or periodical published shall suffice.

§ 21. **Same; Effect of Accidental Omission From Copy or Copies.**—Where the copyright proprietor has sought to comply with the provisions of this title with respect to notice, the omission by accident or mistake of the prescribed notice from a particular copy or copies shall not invalidate the copyright or prevent recovery for infringement against any person who, after actual notice of the copyright, begins an undertaking to infringe it, but shall prevent the recovery of damages against an innocent infringer who has been misled by the omission of the notice; and in a suit for infringement no permanent injunction shall be had unless the copyright proprietor shall reimburse to the innocent infringer his reasonable outlay innocently incurred if the court, in its discretion, shall so direct.

§ 22. **Ad Interim Protection of Book or Periodical Published Abroad.**—In the case of a book or periodical first published abroad in the English language, the deposit in the Copyright Office, not later than six months after its publication abroad, of one complete copy of the foreign edition, with a request for the reservation of the copyright and a statement of the name and nationality of the author and of the copyright proprietor and of the date of publication of the said book or periodical, shall secure to the author or proprietor an ad interim copyright therein, which shall have all the force and effect given to copyright by this title, and shall endure until the expiration of five years after the date of first publication abroad.

§ 23. **Same; Extension to Full Term.**—Whenever within the period of such ad interim protection an authorized edition of such books or periodicals shall be published within the United States, in accordance with the manufacturing provisions specified in section 16 of this title, and whenever the provisions of this title as to deposit of copies, registration, filing of affidavits, and the printing of the copyright notice shall have been duly complied with, the copyright shall be extended to endure in such book or periodical for the term provided in this title.

§ 24. **Duration; Renewal and Extension.**—The copyright secured by this title shall endure for twenty-eight years from the date of first publication, whether the copyrighted work bears the author's true name or is published anonymously or under an assumed name: *Provided,* That in the case of any posthumous work or of any periodical, cyclopedic, or other composite work upon which the copyright was originally secured by the proprietor thereof, or of any work copyrighted by a corporate body (otherwise than as assignee or licensee of the individual author) or by an employer for whom such work is made for hire, the proprietor of such copyright shall be entitled to a renewal and extension of the copyright in such work for the further term of twenty-eight years when application for such renewal and extension shall have been made to the copyright office and duly registered therein within one year prior to the expiration of the original term of copyright: *And provided further,* That in the case of any other copyrighted work, including a contribution by an individual author to a periodical or to a cyclopedic or other composite work, the author of such work, if still living, or the widow, widower, or children of the author, if the author be not living, or if such author, widow, widower, or children be not living, then the author's executors, or in the absence of a will, his next of kin shall be entitled to a renewal and extension of the copyright in such work for a further term of twenty-eight years when application for such renewal and extension shall have been made to the copyright office and duly registered therein within one year prior to the expiration of the original term of copyright: *And provided further,* That in default of the registration of such application for renewal and extension, the copyright in any work shall determine at the expiration of twenty-eight years from first publication.

§ 25. **Renewal of Copyrights Registered in Patent Office Under Repealed Law.**—Subsisting copyrights originally registered in the Patent Office prior to July 1, 1940, under section 3 of the act of June 18, 1874, shall be subject to renewal in behalf of the proprietor upon application made to the Register of Copyrights within one year prior to the expiration of the original term of twenty-eight years.

§ 26. **Terms Defined.**—In the interpretation and construction of this title "the date of publication" shall in the case of a work of which copies are reproduced for sale or distribution be held to be the earliest date when copies of the first authorized edition were placed on sale, sold, or publicly distributed by the proprietor of the copyright or under his authority, and the word "author" shall include an employer in the case of works made for hire.

§ 27. **Copyright Distinct from Property in Object Copyrighted; Effect of Sale of Object and of Assignment of Copyright.**—The copyright is distinct from the property in the material object copyrighted, and the sale or conveyance, by gift or otherwise, of the material object shall not of itself constitute a transfer of the copyright, nor shall the assignment of the copyright constitute a transfer of the title to the material object; but nothing in this title shall be deemed to forbid, prevent, or restrict the transfer of any copy of a copyrighted work the possession of which has been lawfully obtained.

§ 28. **Assignments and Bequests.**—Copyright secured under this title or previous copyright laws of the United States may be assigned, granted, or mortgaged by an instrument in writing signed by the proprietor of the copyright, or may be bequeathed by will.

§ 29. **Same; Executed in Foreign Country; Acknowledgment and Certificate.**—Every assignment of copyright executed in a foreign country shall be acknowledged by the assignor before a consular officer or secretary of legation of the United States authorized by law to administer oaths or perform notarial acts. The certificate of such acknowledgment under the hand and official seal of such consular officer or secretary of legation shall be prima facie evidence of the execution of the instrument.

§ 30. **Same; Record.**—Every assignment of copyright shall be recorded in the copyright office within three calendar months after its execution in the United States or within six calendar months after its execution without the limits of the United States, in default of which it shall be void as against any subsequent purchaser or mortgagee for a valuable consideration, without notice, whose assignment has been duly recorded.

§ 31. **Same; Certificate of Record.**—The Register of Copyrights shall, upon payment of the prescribed fee, record such assignment, and shall return it to the sender with a certificate of record attached under seal of the copyright office, and upon the payment of the fee prescribed by this title he shall furnish to any person requesting the same a certified copy thereof under the said seal.

§ 32. **Same; Use of Name of Assignee in Notice.**—When an assignment of the copyright in a specified book or other work has been recorded the assignee may substitute his name for that of the assignor in the statutory notice of copyright prescribed by this title.

Chapter 2—Infringement proceedings

§ 101. Infringement:
    (a) Injunction.
    (b) Damages and profits; amounts; other remedies.
    (c) Impounding during action.
    (d) Destruction of infringing copies and plates.
    (e) Royalties for use of mechanical reproduction of musical works.

§ 104. Willful infringement for profit.
§ 105. Fraudulent notice of copyright, or removal or alteration of notice.
§ 106. Importation of article bearing false notice or piratical copies of copyrighted work.
§ 107. Importation, during existence of copyright, of piratical copies, or of copies not produced in accordance with section 16 of this title.
§ 108. Forfeiture and destruction of articles prohibited importation.
§ 109. Importation of prohibited articles; regulations; proof of deposit of copies by complainants.
§ 112. Injunctions; service and enforcement.
§ 113. Transmission of certified copies of papers for enforcement of injunction by other court.
§ 114. Review of orders, judgments, or decrees.
§ 115. Limitations.
§ 116. Costs; attorney's fees.

§ 101. **Infringement.**—If any person shall infringe the copyright in any work protected under the copyright laws of the United States such person shall be liable:
    (a) **Injunction.**—To an injunction restraining such infringement;
    (b) **Damages and Profits; Amount; Other Remedies.**—To pay to the

copyright proprietor such damages as the copyright proprietor may have suffered due to the infringement, as well as all the profits which the infringer shall have made from such infringement, and in proving profits the plaintiff shall be required to prove sales only, and the defendant shall be required to prove every element of cost which he claims, or in lieu of actual damages and profits, such damages as to the court shall appear to be just, and in assessing such damages the court may, in its discretion, allow the amounts as hereinafter stated, but in case of a newspaper reproduction of a copyrighted photograph, such damages shall not exceed the sum of $200 nor be less than the sum of $50, and in the case of the infringement of an undramatized or nondramatic work by means of motion pictures, where the infringer shall show that he was not aware that he was infringing, and that such infringement could not have been reasonably foreseen, such damages shall not exceed the sum of $100; and in the case of an infringement of a copyrighted dramatic or dramatico-musical work by a maker of motion pictures and his agencies for distribution thereof to exhibitors, where such infringer shows that he was not aware that he was infringing a copyrighted work, and that such infringements could not reasonably have been foreseen, the entire sum of such damages recoverable by the copyright proprietor from such infringing maker and his agencies for the distribution to exhibitors of such infringing motion picture shall not exceed the sum of $5,000 nor be less than $250, and such damages shall in no other case exceed the sum of $5,000 nor be less than the sum of $250, and shall not be regarded as a penalty. But the foregoing exceptions shall not deprive the copyright proprietor of any other remedy given him under this law, nor shall the limitation as to the amount of recovery apply to infringements occurring after the actual notice to a defendant, either by service of process in a suit or other written notice served upon him.

First. In the case of a painting, statue, or sculpture, $10 for every infringing copy made or sold by or found in the possession of the infringer or his agents or employees;

Second. In the case of any work enumerated in section 5 of this title, except a painting, statue, or sculpture, $1 for every infringing copy made or sold by or found in the possession of the infringer or his agents or employees;

Third. In the case of a lecture, sermon, or address, $50 for every infringing delivery;

Fourth. In the case of a dramatic or dramatico-musical or a choral or orchestral composition, $100 for the first and $50 for every subsequent infringing performance; in the case of other musical compositions $10 for every infringing performance;

(c) **Impounding During Action.**—To deliver up on oath, to be impounded during the pendency of the action, upon such terms and conditions as the court may prescribe, all articles alleged to infringe a copyright;

(d) **Destruction of Infringing Copies and Plates.**—To deliver up on oath for destruction all the infringing copies or devices, as well as all plates, molds, matrices, or other means for making such infringing copies as the court may order.

(e) **Royalties for Use of Mechanical Reproduction of Musical Works.**—Whenever the owner of a musical copyright has used or permitted the use of the copyrighted work upon the parts of musical instruments serving to reproduce mechanically the musical work, then in case of infringement of such copyright by the unauthorized manufacture, use, or sale or interchangeable parts, such as disks, rolls, bands, or cylinders for use in mechanical music-producing machines adapted to reproduce the copyrighted music, no criminal action shall be brought, but in a civil action an injunction may be granted upon such terms as the court may impose, and the plaintiff shall be entitled to recover in lieu of profits and damages a royalty as provided in section 1, subsection (e), of this title: *Provided also,* That whenever any person, in the absence of a license agreement, intends to use a copyrighted musical composition upon the parts of instruments serving to reproduce mechanically the musical work, relying upon the compulsory license provision of this title, he shall serve notice of such intention, by registered mail, upon the copyright proprietor at his last address disclosed by the records of the copyright office, sending to the copyright office a duplicate of such notice; and in case of his failure so to do the court may, in its discretion, in addition to sums hereinabove mentioned, award the complainant a further sum, not to exceed three times the amount provided by section 1, subsection (e), of this title, by way of damages, and not as a penalty, and also a temporary injunction until the full award is paid.

(f) [Repealed 1948]

§ 102. [Repealed 1948]

§ 103. [Repealed 1948]

§ 104. **Willful Infringement for Profit.**—Any person who willfully and for profit shall infringe any copyright secured by this title, or who shall knowingly and willfully aid or abet such infringement, shall be deemed guilty of a misdemeanor, and upon conviction thereof shall be punished by imprisonment for not exceeding one year or by a fine of not less than $100 nor more than $1,000, or both, in the discretion of the court: *Provided, however,* That nothing in this title shall be so construed as to prevent the performance of religious or secular works such as oratorios, cantatas, masses, or octavo choruses by public schools, church choirs, or vocal societies, rented, borrowed, or obtained from some public library, public school, church choir, school choir, or vocal society, provided the performance is given for charitable or educational purposes and not for profit.

§ 105. **Fraudulent Notice of Copyright, or Removal or Alteration of Notice.**—Any person who, with fraudulent intent, shall insert or impress any notice of copyright required by this title, or words of the same purport, in or upon any uncopyrighted article, or with fraudulent intent shall remove or alter the copyright notice upon any article duly copyrighted shall be guilty of a misdemeanor, punishable by a fine of not less than $100 and not more than $1,000. Any person who shall knowingly issue or sell any article bearing a notice of United States copyright which has not been copyrighted in this country, or who shall knowingly import any article bearing such notice or words of the same purport, which has not been copyrighted in this country, shall be liable to a fine of $100.

§ 106. **Importation of Article Bearing False Notice or Piratical Copies of Copyrighted Work.**—The importation into the United States of any article bearing a false notice of copyright when there is no existing copyright thereon in the United States, or of any piratical copies of any work copyrighted in the United States, is prohibited.

§ 107. **Importation, During Existence of Copyright, of Piratical Copies, or of Copies Not Produced in Accordance With Section 16 of This Title.**— During the existence of the American copyright in any book the importation into the United States of any piratical copies thereof or of any copies thereof (although authorized by the author or proprietor) which have not been produced in accordance with the manufacturing provisions specified in section 16 of this title, or any plates of the same not made from type set within the limits of the United States, or any copies thereof produced by lithographic or photoengraving process not performed within the limits of the United States, in accordance with the provisions of section 16 of this title, is prohibited: *Provided, however,* That, except as regards piratical copies, such prohibition shall not apply:

(a) To works in raised characters for the use of the blind.

(b) To a foreign newspaper or magazine, although containing matter copyrighted in the United States printed or reprinted by authority of the copyright proprietor, unless such newspaper or magazine contains also copyright matter printed or reprinted without such authorization.

(c) To the authorized edition of a book in a foreign language or languages of which only a translation into English has been copyrighted in this country.

(d) To any book published abroad with the authorization of the author or copyright proprietor when imported under the circumstances stated in one of the four subdivisions following, that is to say:

First. When imported, not more than one copy at one time, for individual use and not for sale; but such privilege of importation shall not extend to a foreign reprint of a book by an American author copyrighted in the United States.

Second. When imported by the authority or for the use of the United States.

Third. When imported, for use and not for sale, not more than one copy of any such book in any one invoice, in good faith by or for any society or institution incorporated for educational, literary, philosophical, scientific, or religious purposes, or for the encouragement of the fine arts, or for any college, academy, school, or seminary of learning, or for any State, school, college, university, or free public library in the United States.

Fourth. When such books form parts of libraries or collections purchased en bloc for the use of societies, institutions, or libraries designated in the foregoing paragraph, or form parts of the libraries or personal baggage belonging to persons or families arriving from foreign countries and are not intended for sale: *Provided,* That copies imported as above may not lawfully be used in any way to violate the rights of the proprietor of the American copyright or annul or limit the copyright protection secured by this title, and such unlawful use shall be deemed an infringement of copyright.

§ 108. **Forfeiture and Destruction of Articles Prohibited Importation.**—Any and all articles prohibited importation by this title which are brought into the United States from any foreign country (except in the mails) shall be seized and forfeited by like proceedings as those provided by law for the seizure and condemnation of property imported into the United States in violation of the customs revenue laws. Such articles when forfeited shall be destroyed in such manner as the Secretary of the Treasury or the court, as the case may be, shall direct: *Provided, however,* That all copies of authorized editions of copyright books imported in the mails or otherwise in violation of the provisions of this title may be exported and returned to the country of export whenever it is shown to the satisfaction of the Secretary of the Treasury, in a written application, that such importation does not involve willful negligence or fraud.

§ 109. **Importation of Prohibited Articles; Regulations; Proof of Deposit of Copies by Complainants.**—The Secretary of the Treasury and the Postmaster General are hereby empowered and required to make and enforce individually or jointly such rules and regulations as shall prevent the importation into the United States of articles prohibited importation by this title, and may require, as conditions precedent to exclusion of any work in which copyright is claimed, the copyright proprietor or any person claiming actual or potential injury by reason of actual or contemplated importations of copies of such work to file with the Post Office Department or the Treasury Department a certificate of the Register of Copyrights that the provisions of section 13 of this title have been fully complied with, and to give notice of such compliance to postmasters or to customs officers at the ports of entry in the United States in such form and accompanied by such exhibits as may be deemed necessary for the practical and efficient administration and enforcement of the provisions of sections 106 and 107 of this title.

§ 110. [Repealed 1948]

§ 111. [Repealed 1948]

§ 112. **Injunctions; Service and Enforcement.**—Any court mentioned in section 1338 of Title 28 or judge thereof shall have power, upon complaint filed by any party aggrieved, to grant injunctions to prevent and restrain the violation of any right secured by this title, according to the course and principles of courts of equity, on such terms as said court or judge may deem reasonable. Any injunction that may be granted restraining and enjoining the doing of anything forbidden by this title may be served on the parties against whom such injunction may be granted anywhere in the United States, and shall be operative throughout the United States and be enforceable by proceedings in contempt or otherwise by any other court or judge possessing jurisdiction of the defendants.

§ 113. **Transmission of Certified Copies of Papers for Enforcement of Injunction by Other Court.**—The clerk of the court, or judge granting the injunction, shall, when required so to do by the court hearing the application to enforce said injunction, transmit without delay to said court a certified copy of all the papers in said cause that are on file in his office.

§ 114. **Review of Orders, Judgments, or Decrees.**—The orders, judgments, or decrees of any court mentioned in section 1338 of Title 28 arising under the copyright laws of the United States may be reviewed on appeal in the manner and to the extent now provided by law for the review of cases determined in said courts, respectively.

§ 115. **Limitations.**—(a) **Criminal Proceedings.**—No criminal proceedings shall be maintained under the provisions of this title unless the same is commenced within three years after the cause of action arose.

(b) Civil Actions.—No civil action shall be maintained under the provisions of this title unless the same is commenced within three years after the claim accrued.

§116. **Costs; Attorney's Fees.**—In all actions, suits, or proceedings under this title, except when brought by or against the United States or any officer thereof, full costs shall be allowed, and the court may award to the prevailing party a reasonable attorney's fee as part of the costs.

Chapter 3—Copyright office

§ 201. **Copyright Office; Preservation of Records.**—All records and other things relating to copyrights required by law to be preserved shall be kept and preserved in the copyright office, Library of Congress, District of Columbia, and shall be under the control of the register of copyrights, who shall, under the direction and supervision of the Librarian of Congress, perform all the duties relating to the registration of copyrights.

§ 202. **Register, Assistant Register, and Subordinates.**—There shall be appointed by the Librarian of Congress a Register of Copyrights, and one Assistant Register of Copyrights, who shall have authority during the absence of the Register of Copyrights to attach the copyright office seal to all papers issued from the said office and to sign such certificates and other papers as may be necessary. There shall also be appointed by the Librarian such subordinate assistants to the register as may from time to time be authorized by law.

§ 203. **Same; Deposit of Moneys Received; Reports.**—The Register of Copyrights shall make daily deposits in some bank in the District of Columbia, designated for this purpose by the Secretary of the Treasury as a national depository, of all moneys received to be applied as copyright fees, and shall make weekly deposits with the Secretary of the Treasury, in such manner as the latter shall direct, of all copyright fees actually applied under the provisions of this title, and annual deposits of sums received which it has not been possible to apply as copyright fees or to return to the remitters, and shall also make monthly reports to the Secretary of the Treasury and to the Librarian of Congress of the applied copyright fees for each calendar month, together with a statement of all remittances received, trust funds on hand, moneys refunded, and unapplied balances.

§ 204. **Same; Bond.**—The Register of Copyrights shall give bond to the United States in the sum of $20,000, in form to be approved by the General Counsel for the Department of the Treasury and with sureties satisfactory to the Secretary of the Treasury, for the faithful discharge of his duties.

§ 205. **Same; Annual report.**—The Register of Copyrights shall make an annual report to the Librarian of Congress, to be printed in the annual report on the Library of Congress, of all copyright business for the previous fiscal year, including the number and kind of works which have been deposited in the copyright office during the fiscal year, under the provisions of this title.

§ 206. **Seal of Copyright Office.**—The seal used in the copyright office on July 1, 1909, shall be the seal of the copyright office, and by it all papers issued from the copyright office requiring authentication shall be authenticated.

§ 207. **Rules for Registration of Claims.**—Subject to the approval of the Librarian of Congress, the Register of Copyrights shall be authorized to make rules and regulations for the registration of claims to copyright as provided by this title.

§ 208. **Record Books in Copyright Office.**—The Register of Copyrights shall provide and keep such record books in the copyright office as are required to carry out the provisions of this title, and whenever deposit has been made in the copyright office of a copy of any work under the provisions of this title he shall make entry thereof.

209. **Certificate of Registration; Effect as Evidence; Receipt for Copies Deposited.**—In the case of each entry the person recorded as the claimant of the copyright shall be entitled to a certificate of registration under seal of the copyright office, to contain the name and address of said claimant, the name of the country of which the author of the work is a citizen or subject, and when an alien author domiciled in the United States at the time of said registration, then a statement of that fact, including his place of domicile, the name of the author (when the records of the copyright office shall show the same), the title of the work which is registered for which copyright is claimed, the date of the deposit of the copies of such work, the date of publication if the work has been reproduced in copies for sale, or publicly distributed, and such marks as to class designation and entry number as shall fully identify the entry. In the case of a book, the certificate shall also state the receipt of the affidavit, as provided by section 17 of this title, and the date of the completion of the printing, or the date of the publication of the book, as stated in the said affidavit. The Register of Copyrights shall prepare a printed form for the said certificate, to be filled out in each case as above provided for in the case of all registrations made after July 1, 1909, and in the case of all previous registrations so far as the copyright office record books shall show such facts, which certificate, sealed with the seal of the copyright office, shall, upon payment of the prescribed fee, be given to any person making application for the same. Said certificate shall be admitted in any court as prima facie evidence of the facts stated therein. In addition to such certificate the register of copyrights shall furnish, upon request, without additional fee, a receipt for the copies of the work deposited to complete the registration.

§ 210. **Catalog of Copyright Entries; Effect as Evidence.**—The Register of Copyrights shall fully index all copyright registrations and assignments and shall print at periodic intervals a catalog of the titles of articles deposited and registered for copyright, together with suitable indexes, and at stated intervals shall print complete and indexed catalog for each class of copyright entries, and may thereupon, if expedient, destroy the original manuscript catalog cards containing the titles included in such printed volumes and representing the entries made during such intervals. The current catalog of copyright entries and the index volumes herein provided for shall be admitted in any court as prima facie evidence of the facts stated therein as regards any copyright registration.

§ 211. **Same; Distribution and Sale; Disposal of Proceeds.**—The said printed current catalogs as they are issued shall be promptly distributed by the Superintendent of Documents to the collectors of customs of the United States and to the postmasters of all exchange offices of receipt of foreign mails, in accordance with revised list of such collectors of customs and postmasters prepared by the Secretary of the Treasury and the Postmaster General, and they shall also be furnished in whole or in part to all parties desiring them at a price to be determined by the Register of Copyrights for each part of the catalog not exceeding $25 for the complete yearly catalog of copyright entries. The consolidated catalogs and indexes shall also be supplied to all persons ordering them at such prices as may be fixed by the Register of Copyrights, and all subscriptions for the catalogs shall be received by the Superintendent of Documents, who shall forward the said publications; and the moneys thus received shall be paid into the Treasury of the United States and accounted for under such laws and Treasury regulations as shall be in force at the time.

§ 212. **Records and Works Deposited in Copyright Office Open to Public Inspection; Taking Copies of Entries.**—The record books of the copyright office, together with the indexes to such record books, and all works deposited and retained in the copyright office, shall be open to public inspection; and copies may be taken of the copyright entries actually made in such record books, subject to such safeguards and regulations as shall be prescribed by the Register of Copyrights and approved by the Librarian of Congress.

§ 213. **Disposition of Articles Deposited in Office.**—Of the articles deposited in the copyright office under the provisions of the copyright laws of the United States, the Librarian of Congress shall determine what books and other articles shall be transferred to the permanent collections of the Library of Congress, including the law library, and what other books or articles shall be placed in the reserve collections of the Library of Congress for sale or exchange, or be transferred to other governmental libraries in the District of Columbia for use therein.

§ 214. **Destruction of Articles Deposited in Office Remaining Undisposed of; Removal of by Author or Proprietor; Manuscripts of Unpublished Works.**—Of any articles undisposed of as above provided, together with all titles and correspondence relating thereto, the Librarian of Congress and the Register of Copyrights jointly shall, at suitable intervals, determine what of these received during any period of years it is desirable or useful to preserve in the permanent files of the copyright office, and, after due notice as hereinafter provided, may within their discretion cause the remaining articles and other things to be destroyed: *Provided,* That there shall be printed in the Catalog of Copyright Entries from February to November, inclusive, a statement of the years of receipt of such articles and a notice to permit any author, copyright proprietor, or other lawful claimant to claim and remove before the expiration of the month of December of that year anything found which relates to any of his productions deposited or registered for copyright within the period of years stated, not reserved or disposed of as provided for in this title. No manuscript of an unpublished work shall be destroyed during its term of copyright without specific notice to the copyright proprietor of record, permitting him to claim and remove it.

§ 215. **Fees.**—The Register of Copyrights shall receive, and the persons to whom the services designated are rendered shall pay, the following fees:

For the registration of a claim to copyright in any work, except a print or label used for articles of merchandise, $4; for the registration of a claim to copyright in a print or label used for articles of merchandise, $6; which fees shall include a certificate of registration under seal for each work registered: *Provided,* That only one registration fee shall be required in the case of several volumes of the same book published and deposited at the same time: *And provided further,* That with respect to works of foreign origin, in lieu of payment of the copyright fee of $4 together with one copy of the work and application, the foreign author or proprietor may at any time within six months from the date of first publication abroad deposit in the Copyright Office an application for registration and two copies of the work which shall be accompanied by a catalog card in form and content satisfactory to the Register of Copyrights.

For recording the renewal of copyright and issuance of certificate therefor, $2.

For every additional certificate of registration, $1.

For certifying a copy of an application for registration of copyright, and for all other certifications, $2.

For recording every assignment, agreement, power of attorney, or other paper not exceeding six pages, $3; for each additional page or less, 50 cents; for each title over one in the paper recorded, 50 cents additional.

For recording a notice of use, $2, for each notice of not more than five titles; and 50 cents for each additional title.

For any requested search of Copyright Office records, or works deposited, or services rendered in connection therewith, $3 for each hour of time consumed.

§ 216. **When the Day for Taking Action Falls on Saturday, Sunday, or**

a Holiday.—When the last day for making any deposit or application, or for paying any fee, or for delivering any other material to the Copyright Office falls on Saturday, Sunday, or a holiday within the District of Columbia, such action may be taken on the next succeeding business day.

Appendix B

Regulations of the Copyright Office[1]

Part 201—General Provisions

Sec.

201.1 Communications with the Copyright Office.
201.2 Information given by the Copyright Office.
201.3 Catalog of Copyright Entries.
201.4 Assignments of copyright and other papers.
201.5 Amendments to completed Copyright Office registrations and other records.
201.6 Payment and refund of Copyright Office fees.
201.7 Preparation of catalog card.
201.8 Import statements.

AUTHORITY: §§ 201.1 to 201.8 issued under sec. 207, 61 Stat. 666; 17 U.S.C. 207.

§ 201.1. **Communications with the Copyright Office.**—Mail and other communications shall be addressed to the Register of Copyrights, Library of Congress, Washington 25, D.C.

§ 201.2. **Information Given by the Copyright Office.**—(a) *In general.* (1) Information relative to the operations of the Copyright Office is supplied without charge. A search of the records, indexes and deposits will be made for such information as they may contain relative to copyright claims upon application and payment of the statutory fee. The Copyright Office, however, does not undertake the making of comparisons of copyright deposits to determine similarity between works, nor does it give legal opinions or advice on such matters as:

---

[1] *Code of Federal Regulations*, Title 37, Chapter II (24 F.R. 4955).
(In effect as of June 18, 1959)

(i) The validity or status of any copyright other than the facts shown in the records of the Office;

(ii) The rights of persons, whether in connection with cases of alleged copyright infringement, contracts between authors and publishers, or other matters of a similar nature;

(iii) The scope and extent of protection of works in foreign countries or interpretation of foreign copyright laws or court opinions;

(iv) The sufficiency, extent, or scope of compliance with the copyright law.

(2) In addition, the Office cannot undertake to furnish the names of copyright attorneys, publishers, agents, or other similar information.

(b) *Inspection and copying of records.* (1) Inspection and copying of completed records and indexes relating to a registration or a recorded document, and inspection of copies deposited in connection with a completed copyright registration, may be undertaken at such times as will not result in interference with or delay in the work of the Copyright Office.

(2) The copying from the Copyright Office records of names and addresses for the purpose of compiling mailing lists and other similar uses is expressly prohibited.

(c) *Correspondence.* (1) Official correspondence, including preliminary applications, between copyright claimants or their agents and the Copyright Office, and directly relating to a completed registration or to a recorded document, is made available for inspection by persons properly and directly concerned. Requests for photocopies of the correspondence shall be made pursuant to paragraph (d) of this section.

(2) (i) Correspondence, application forms and any accompanying material forming a part of a pending or rejected application are not records which are open to public inspection under paragraph (b) of this section.

(ii) Inspection of such files may be afforded upon presentation of written authorization of the claimant or his agent, or upon submission to the Register of Copyrights, Library of Congress, Washington 25, D.C., of a written request which is deemed by him to show good cause for such access and which establishes that the person making the request is one properly and directly concerned.

(iii) Where such access is authorized and photocopies of the official file are subsequently requested, the conditions and procedures of paragraph (d) of this section are controlling.

(3) Correspondence, memoranda, reports, opinions, and similar material relating to internal management, office administration, security matters, and general policy and decisional material, including the work product of an attorney, are not open to public inspection.

(4) The Copyright Office will return unanswered any abusive or scurrilous correspondence.

(d) *Requests for copies.* (1) Requests for additional certificates of registration should be sent to the Copyright Office, and the accompanying fees should be made payable to the Register of Copyrights.

(2) Requests for photocopies of copyright deposits, official correspondence, and Copyright Office records (other than additional certificates of registration) should be sent to the Chief, Photoduplication Service, Library of Congress, Washington 25, D.C., the accompanying fees in payment of such services being made payable to that official. When the photocopy is to be certified by the Copyright Office, the additional certification fee should be made payable to the Register of Copyrights and both remittances together with the transmittal letter are to be sent to the Copyright Office.

(3) Requests for photocopies of official correspondence shall identify the specific material desired and shall contain a statement enabling the Copyright Office to determine if the writer is properly and directly concerned.

(4) Requests for photocopies of copyright deposits will be granted when one or more of the following conditions are fulfilled:

(i) *Authorization by owner.* When authorized in writing by the copyright owner or his designated agent.

(ii) *Request by attorney.* When required in connection with litigation, actual or prospective, in which the copyrighted work is involved; but in all such cases the attorney representing the actual or prospective plaintiff or defendant for whom the request is made shall give in writing: (*a*) The names of the parties and the nature of the controversy; (*b*) the name of the court where the action is pending, or, in the case of a prospective proceeding, a full statement of the facts of the controversy in which the copyrighted work is involved; and (*c*) satisfactory assurances that the requested copy will be used only in connection with the specified litigation.

(iii) *Court order.* When an order to have the copy made is issued by a court having jurisdiction of a case in which the copy is to be submitted as evidence.

§ 201.3. **Catalog of Copyright Entries.**—The current subscription price for all parts of the complete yearly Catalog of Copyright Entries is $20.00. Each part of the Catalog is published in two semiannual numbers covering, respectively, the periods January-June and July-December. The prices given in the list below are for each semiannual number. The Catalog may be obtained, upon payment of the established price, from the Register of Copyrights, Library of Congress, Washington 25, D.C., to whom requests for copies should be addressed and to whom the remittance should be made payable.

Part 1—Books and Pamphlets, Including Serials and Contributions to Periodicals, $2.50.
Part 2—Periodicals, $1.00.

Parts 3-4—Dramas and Works Prepared for Oral Delivery, $1.00.
Part 5—Music, $3.50.
Part 6—Maps and Atlases, $0.50.
Parts 7-11A—Works of Art, Reproductions of Works of Art, Scientific and Technical Drawings, Photographic Works, Prints and Pictorial Illustrations, $1.00.
Part 11B—Commercial Prints and Labels, $1.00.
Parts 12-13—Motion Pictures and Filmstrips, $0.50.

§ 201.4. **Assignments of Copyright and Other Papers.**—Assignments of copyright and other papers relative to copyrights will be recorded in the Copyright Office upon payment of the statutory fee. Examples of such papers include powers of attorney, licenses to use a copyrighted work, agreements between authors and publishers covering a particular work or works and the rights thereto, mortgages, certificates of change of corporate title, wills, and decrees of distribution. The original, signed instrument should be submitted for recordation, and is returned to the sender with a certificate of record. Where the original instrument is not available, a certified or other copy may be submitted, but it shall be accompanied by a statement that the original is not available.

§ 201.5. **Amendments to Completed Copyright Office Registrations and Other Records.**—(a) *No cancellations.* No correction or cancellation of a Copyright Office registration or other record will be made (other than a registration or record provisional upon receipt of fee as provided in § 201.6) after it has been completed if the facts therein stated agree with those supplied the Office for the purpose of making such record. However, it shall be within the discretion of the Register of Copyrights to determine if any particular case justifies the placing of an annotation upon any record for the purpose of clarification, explanation, or indication that there exists elsewhere in the records, indexes, or correspondence files of the Office, information which has reference to the facts as stated in such record.

(b) *Correction by new registration.* In exceptional cases, where an applicant desires to correct, amend or amplify a registration previously made in accordance with information furnished by a claimant or his agent, a new application indicating its amendatory purpose shall be filed, accompanied by the statutory fee and the same number of copies required for a new application. Where it is satisfactorily established that copies of the original work cannot be obtained for submission, photostat or microfilm copies of the original may be submitted.

§ 201.6. **Payment and Refund of Copyright Office Fees.**—(a) *In general.* All fees sent to the Copyright Office should be in the form of a money order, check or bank draft payable to the Register of Copyrights. Coin or currency sent to the Office in letters or packages will be at the remitter's risk. Remittances from foreign countries should be in the form of an International Money Order or Bank Draft payable and immediately negotiable in the United States for the full amount of the fee required.

Uncertified checks are accepted subject to collection. Where the statutory fee is submitted in the form of a check, the registration of the copyright claim or other record made by the Office is provisional until payment in money is received. In the event the fee is not paid, the registration or other record shall be expunged.

(b) *Deposit accounts.* Persons or firms having a considerable amount of business with the Copyright Office may, for their own convenience, prepay copyright expenses by establishing a Deposit Account.

(c) *Refunds.* Money paid for applications which are rejected or payments made in excess of the statutory fee will be refunded, but amounts of twenty-five cents or less will not be returned unless specifically requested and such sums may be refunded in postage stamps. All larger amounts will be refunded by check.

(d) *Return of deposit copies.* Copies of works deposited in the Copyright Office pursuant to law are either retained in the Copyright Office, transferred for the permanent collections or other uses of the Library of Congress, or disposed of according to law. When an application is rejected, the Copyright Office reserves the right to retain the deposited copies.

§ 201.7. **Preparation of Catalog Card.**—The catalog card which may accompany a work of foreign origin, as provided in section 215 of title 17, U.S. Code, as amended, may be a catalog card supplied by a library in the country of publication. In lieu of such a card the applicant may prepare his own card, or may fill out the form supplied by the Copyright Office. The catalog card should contain the full name of the author of the original work, title and description from the title page, paging, copyright claimant, the city and year of publication, and the names of all other authors, editors, etc., whom the applicant considers of sufficient importance to record. When available, the year of birth of each author named should be given. If the form furnished by the Office is not used, the size of the card should preferably be 5 inches wide by 3 inches deep or 12.5 centimeters wide by 7.5 centimeters deep. The Register of Copyrights reserves the right to accept catalog cards not complying with the above requirements.

§ 201.8. **Import Statements.**—(a) The Copyright Office will issue import statements for books and periodicals first published abroad in the English language which are to be imported under the provisions of section 16 of title 17, U.S. Code, as amended. A statement for the importation of 1,500 copies will be issued to the person named in the application for ad interim copyright registration. The holder of this statement shall present it to the customs officer in charge of the port of entry. Upon receipt of a statement from the customs officer, showing importation of less than 1,500 copies, a new statement will be issued for the balance.

(b) The provisions in the Customs Regulations covering the use of the import statement (Copyright Office Form C-85) are found in 19 CFR 11.21 (21 F.R. 2517).

**Part 202—Registration of
Claims to Copyright**

AUTHORITY: §§ 202.1 to 202.18 issued under sec. 207, 61 Stat. 666; 17 U.S.C. 207.

§ 202.1. **Material Not Subject to Copyright.**—The following are examples of works not subject to copyright and applications for registration of such works cannot be entertained:

(a) Words and short phrases such as names, titles, and slogans; familiar symbols or designs; mere variations of typographic ornamentation, lettering or coloring; mere listing of ingredients or contents;

(b) Ideas, plans, methods, systems, or devices, as distinguished from the particular manner in which they are expressed or described in a writing;

(c) Works designed for recording information which do not in themselves convey information, such as time cards, graph paper, account books, diaries, bank checks, score cards, address books, report forms, order forms and the like;

(d) Works consisting entirely of information that is common property containing no original authorship, such as, for example: Standard calendars, height and weight charts, tape measures and rulers, schedules of sporting events, and lists or tables taken from public documents or other common sources.

§ 202.2. **Copyright Notice.**—(a) *General.* (1) With respect to a published work, copyright is secured, or the right to secure it is lost, at the date of publication, i.e., the date on which copies are first placed on sale, sold, or publicly distributed, depending upon the adequacy of the notice of copyright on the work at that time.

(2) If publication occurs by distribution of copies or in some other manner, without the statutory notice or with an inadequate notice, the right to secure copyright is lost. In such cases, copyright cannot be secured by adding the notice to copies distributed at a later date.

(3) Works first published abroad, other than works eligible for ad interim registration, must bear an adequate copyright notice at the time of their first publication in order to secure copyright under the law of the United States.

(b) *Defects in notice.* Where the copyright notice does not meet the requirements of the law, the Copyright Office will reject an application for copyright registration. Common defects in the notice include, among others, the following:

(1) The notice lacks one or more of the necessary elements (i.e., the word "Copyright," the abbreviation "Copr.," or the symbol ©; the name of the copyright proprietor; or, when required, the year date of publication);

(2) The elements of the notice are dispersed;

(3) The notice is not in one of the positions prescribed by law;

(4) The notice is in a foreign language;

(5) The name in the notice is that of someone who had no authority to secure copyright in his name;

(6) The year date in the copyright notice is later than the date of the year in which copyright was actually secured, including the following cases:

(i) Where the year date in the notice is later than the date of actual publication;

(ii) Where copyright was first secured by registration of a work in unpublished form, and copies of the same work as later published without change in substance bear a copyright notice containing a year date later than the year of unpublished registration;

(iii) Where a book or periodical published abroad, for which ad interim copyright has been obtained, is later published in the United States without change in substance and contains a year date in the copyright notice later than the year of first publication abroad: *Provided, however,* That in each of the three foregoing types of cases, if the copyright was actually secured not more than one year earlier than the year date in the notice, registration may be considered as a doubtful case.

(7) A notice is permanently covered so that it cannot be seen without tearing the work apart;

(8) A notice is illegible or so small that it cannot be read without the aid of a magnifying glass: *Provided, however,* That where the work itself requires magnification for its ordinary use (e.g., a microfilm, microcard or motion picture) a notice which will be readable when so magnified, will not constitute a reason for rejection of the claim;

(9) A notice is on a detachable tag and will eventually be detached and discarded when the work is put in use;

(10) A notice is on the wrapper or container which is not a part of the work and which will eventually be removed and discarded when the work is put in use;

(11) The notice is restricted or limited exclusively to an uncopyrightable element, either by virtue of its position on the work, by the use of asterisks or by other means.

§ 202.3. **Application Forms.**—(a) *In general.* Section 5 of title 17 of the U.S. Code provides thirteen classes (Class A through Class M) of works in which copyright may be claimed. Examples of certain works falling within these classes are given in §§ 202.4 to 202.15 inclusive, for the purpose of assisting persons, who desire to obtain registration of a claim to copyright, to select the correct application form.

(b) *Claims of copyright.* (1) All works deposited for registration shall be accompanied by a "claim of copyright" in the form of a properly executed application, together with the statutory registration fee. The Office reserves the right to refuse to accept any application that is a carbon copy, illegible, defaced, or otherwise not in an acceptable condition for examination and recording.

(2) Where these separate elements are not received simultaneously, the Copyright Office holds the submitted elements for a reasonable time and, in default of the receipt of the missing element or elements after a request made therefor, the submitted item or items may be returned to the sender. Such action does not constitute a waiver of the right of the Register of Copyrights pursuant to section 14, title 17, U.S. Code, to demand compliance with the deposit provisions of that title.

(3) Applications for copyright registration covering published works should reflect the facts existing at the time of first publication, and should not include information concerning changes that have occurred between the time of publication and registration. The name given as copyright claimant in the application should agree with the name appearing in the copyright notice.

(4) Applications should be submitted by the copyright claimant, or by someone acting under his authority.

(5) All information requested by the Copyright Office application form should be given in the appropriate spaces provided. There should not be attached to the application any slips of paper or extra pages containing additional information, or a continuation of requested information.

(c) *Forms.* The Copyright Office supplies without charge the following forms for use when applying for the registration of a claim to copyright in a work and for the filing of a notice of use of musical compositions on mechanical instruments.

Form A—Published book manufactured in the United States of America (Class A).

Form A-B Ad Interim—Book or periodical in the English language manufactured and first published outside the United States of America (Classes A-B).

Form A-B Foreign—Book or periodical manufactured outside the United States of America (except works subject to the ad interim provisions of the copyright law) (Classes A-B).

Form B—Periodical manufactured in the United States of America (Class B).

Form BB—Contribution to a periodical manufactured in the United States of America (Class B).

Form C—Lecture or similar production prepared for oral delivery (Class C).

Form D—Dramatic or dramatico-musical composition (Class D).

Form E—Musical composition the author of which is a citizen or domiciliary of the United States of America or which was published in the United States of America (Class E).

Form E Foreign—Musical composition the author of which is not a citizen or domiciliary of the United States of America and which was not first published in the United States of America (Class E).

Form F—Map (Class F).

Form G—Work of art or a model or design for a work of art (Class G).

Form H—Reproduction of a work of art (Class H).

Form I—Drawing or plastic work of a scientific or technical character (Class I).

Form J—Photograph (Class J).

Form K—Print or pictorial illustration (Class K).

Form KK—Print or label used for an article of merchandise (Class K).

Form L-M—Motion picture (Classes L-M).

Form R—Renewal copyright.

Form U—Notice of use of copyrighted music on mechanical instruments.

§ 202.4. **Books (Class A).**—(a) *Subject matter and forms.* This class includes such published works as fiction and nonfiction, poems, compilations, composite works, directories, catalogs, annual publications, information in tabular form, and similar text matter, with or without illustrations, as books, either bound or in loose-leaf form, pamphlets, leaflets, cards, single pages, or the like. Applications for registration of claims to copyright in published books manufactured in the United States of America are made on Form A; in books manufactured outside of the United States of America, except those subject to ad interim provisions of the copyright law, on Form A-B Foreign; and in books in the English language manufactured and first published outside the United States of America, and subject to the ad interim provisions of the copyright law, on Form A-B Ad Interim.

(b) *Ad interim registrations.* (1) An American edition of an English-language book or periodical identical in substance to that first published abroad will not be registered unless an ad interim registration is first made.

(2) When a book or periodical has been registered under the ad interim provisions, an American edition of the same work, to be registrable, must be manufactured and published in the United States within five years after the date of first publication abroad.

(3) Since by law ad interim copyright expires at the end of the ad interim term unless an American edition is published during that term, a renewal application covering a work registered only under the ad interim provisions will be rejected. Where both an ad interim and an American edition have been registered, the registrability of the renewal application is governed by the date of the first publication abroad.

§ 202.5. **Periodicals (Class B).**—This class includes such works as newspapers, magazines, reviews, bulletins, and serial publications, published at intervals of less than a year. Applications for registration of claims to copyright in published periodicals manufactured in the United States of America are made on Form B; in periodicals, or in contributions thereto, manufactured outside the United States of America, except those subject to the ad interim provision of the copyright law, on Form A-B Foreign; and in periodicals, or in contributions thereto, in the English language manufactured and first published outside of the United States of America, and subject to the ad interim provisions of the copyright law, on Form A-B Ad Interim. Applications for registration of claims to copyright in contributions to periodicals manufactured in the United States of America are made on Form BB. Application for registration of claims to copyright in contributions to periodicals, which contributions are prints published in connection with the sale or advertisement of an article or articles of merchandise, are made on Form KK.

§ 202.6. **Lectures or Similar Productions Prepared for Oral Delivery (Class C).**—This class includes the scripts of unpublished works prepared in the first instance for oral delivery, such as lectures, sermons, addresses, monologs, panel discussions, and variety programs prepared for radio or television. The script submitted for registration in Class C should consist of the actual text of the works to be presented orally. Formats, outlines, brochures, synopses, or general descriptions of radio and television programs are not registrable in unpublished form. When published with notice as prescribed by law, such works may be considered for registration as "books" in Class A.

§ 202.7. **Dramatic and Dramatico-Musical Compositions (Class D).—** This class includes published or unpublished works dramatic in character such as the acting version of plays for the stage, motion pictures, radio, television and the like, operas, operettas, musical comedies and similar productions, and pantomimes. Choreographic works of a dramatic character, whether the story or theme be expressed by music and action combined or by actions alone, are subject to registration in Class D. However, descriptions of dance steps and other physical gestures, including ballroom and social dances or choreographic works which do not tell a story, develop a character or emotion, or otherwise convey a dramatic concept or idea, are not subject to registration in Class D.

§ 202.8. **Musical Compositions (Class E).—** (a) This class includes published or unpublished musical compositions in the form of visible notation (other than dramatico-musical compositions), with or without words, as well as new versions of musical compositions, such as adaptations or arrangements, and editing when such editing is the writing of an author. The words of a song, when unaccompanied by music, are not registrable in Class E.

(b) A phonograph record or other sound recording is not considered a "copy" of the compositions recorded on it, and is not acceptable for copyright registration. Likewise, the Copyright Office does not register claims to exclusive rights in mechanical recordings themselves, or in the performances they reproduce.

§ 202.9. **Maps (Class F).—**This class includes all published cartographic representations of area, such as terrestrial maps and atlases, marine charts, celestial maps, and such three-dimensional works as globes and relief models.

§ 202.10. **Works of Art (Class G).—** (a) *General.* This class includes published or unpublished works of artistic craftsmanship, insofar as their form but not their mechanical or utilitarian aspects are concerned, such as artistic jewelry, enamels, glassware, and tapestries, as well as works belonging to the fine arts, such as paintings, drawings and sculpture.

(b) In order to be acceptable as a work of art, the work must embody some creative authorship in its delineation or form. The registrability of a work of art is not affected by the intention of the author as to the use of the work, the number of copies reproduced, or the fact that it appears on a textile material or textile product. The potential availability of protection under the design patent law will not affect the registrability of a work of art, but a copyright claim in a patented design or in the drawings or photographs in a patent application will not be registered after the patent has been issued.

(c) If the sole intrinsic function of an article is its utility, the fact that the article is unique and attractively shaped will not qualify it as a work of art. However, if the shape of a utilitarian article incorporates features, such as artistic sculpture, carving, or pictorial representation, which can be identified separately and are capable of existing independently as a work of art, such features will be eligible for registration.

§ 202.11. **Reproductions of Works of Art (Class H).**—This class includes published reproductions of existing works of art in the same or a different medium, such as a lithograph, photoengraving, etching or drawing of a painting, sculpture, or other work of art.

§ 202.12. **Drawings or Plastic Works of a Scientific or Technical Character (Class I).**—(a) This class includes published or unpublished two-dimensional drawings and three-dimensional plastic works which have been designed for a scientific or technical use and which contain copyrightable graphic, pictorial, or sculptured material. Works registrable in Class I include diagrams or models illustrating scientific or technical works or formulating scientific or technical information in linear or plastic form, such as, for example: a mechanical drawing, an astronomical chart, an architect's blueprint, an anatomical model, or an engineering diagram.

(b) A work is not eligible for registration as a "plastic" work in Class I merely because it is formed from one of the commonly known synthetic chemical derivatives such as styrenes, vinyl compounds, or acrylic resins. The term "plastic work" as used in this context refers to a three-dimensional work giving the effect of that which is molded or sculptured. Examples of such works include statues of animals or plants used for scientific or educational purposes, and engineers' scale models.

(c) A claim to copyright in a scientific or technical drawing, otherwise registrable in Class I, will not be refused registration solely by reason of the fact that it is known to form a part of a pending patent application. Where the patent has been issued, however, the claim to copyright in the drawing will be denied copyright registration.

§ 202.13. **Photographs (Class J).**—This class includes published or unpublished photographic prints and filmstrips, slide films and individual slides. Photoengravings and other photomechanical reproductions of photographs are registered in Class K on Form K.

§ 202.14. **Prints, Pictorial Illustrations and Commercial Prints or Labels (Class K).**—(a) This class includes prints or pictorial illustrations, greeting cards, picture postcards and similar prints, produced by means of lithography, photoengraving or other methods of reproduction. These works when published are registered on Form K.

(b) A print or label, not a trademark, containing copyrightable pictorial matter, text, or both, published in connection with the sale or advertisement of an article or articles of merchandise is also registered in this class on Form KK. In the case of a print which is published in a periodical, use Form KK if the print is used in connection with the sale or advertisement of an article of merchandise, Form BB if it is not. Multipage works are more appropriately classified in Class A than in Class K.

(c) A claim to copyright cannot be registered in a print or label consisting solely of trademark subject matter and lacking copyrightable matter. While the Copyright Office will not investigate whether the matter has been or can be registered at the Patent Office, it will register a properly filed copyright claim in a print or label that contains the requisite qualifications for copyright even though there is a trademark on it. However, registration of a claim to copyright does not give the claimant rights available by trademark registrations at the Patent Office.

§ 202.15. **Motion Pictures (Classes L-M).**—A single application Form L-M is available for registration of works in Classes L (Motion Picture Photoplays) and M (Motion Pictures other than Photoplays).

(a) *Photoplays (Class L).* This class includes published or unpublished motion pictures that are dramatic in character and tell a connected story, such as feature films, filmed television plays, short subjects, and animated cartoons having a plot.

(b) *Other than photoplays (Class M).* This class includes published or unpublished nondramatic films, such as newsreels, travelogs, training or promotional films, nature studies, and filmed television programs having no plot.

§ 202.16. **Deposit of Photographs or Other Identifying Reproductions in Lieu of Copies.**— (a) *Availability of option.* In the case of a published work which is reproduced in copies for sale, classified in Classes (g), (h), (i), and (k) of section 5, title 17, U.S. Code, copies of which are considered by the Register of Copyrights to be impracticable of deposit because of their size, weight, fragility, or monetary value, photographs or other identifying reproductions may be deposited in lieu of copies as provided by section 13, title 17, U.S. Code. The deposit of such photographs or reproductions shall be made in accordance with the following criteria:

(1) The number of sets of photographs or of reproductions to be submitted shall be the same as the number of copies provided by said section 13; duplicate sets shall be deposited unless the work is by a foreign author and has been published in a foreign country. Each set shall consist of as many photographs or reproductions in black and white, or in color, as are necessary to identify the work.

(2) All photographs or reproductions shall be of equal size, not less than 5 x 7 inches, and not exceeding 9 x 12 inches, but preferably 8 x 10 inches. The image of the work shown in all photographs or reproductions shall either be lifesize or larger, or if less than lifesize shall be at least 4 inches in its greatest dimension. The exact measurement of at least one dimension of the work shall be indicated on at least one corresponding photograph or reproduction in each set.

(3) The copyright notice and its position on the work must be clearly shown on at least one corresponding photograph or reproduction in each set. If, because of the size or location of the copyright notice, a photographic reproduction cannot be prepared, a drawing

may be included in each set, of the same size as the photographs or reproductions, showing the exact appearance of the notice, its dimensions, and its specific position on the work.

(4) The title of the work shall appear on the front or back of each photograph or reproduction.

(5) A copy shall be considered to be impracticable of deposit if, because of its size, weight, fragility or monetary value, it is unsuited to the filing procedures of the Copyright Office.

(b) *Exceptions.* The provisions of this section, permitting the deposit of photographs in lieu of copies in certain cases, shall not apply to fine prints and two-dimensional art reproductions. The Register of Copyrights reserves the right in any other particular case to require as a condition precedent to registration, the deposit of copies of the work as published.

§ 202.17. **Renewals.**— (a) Claims to renewal copyright must be registered within the last (28th) year of the original copyright term. The original term for a published work is computed from the date of first publication; the term for a work originally registered in unpublished form is computed from the date of registration in the Copyright Office. Unless the required application and fee are received in the Copyright Office during the prescribed period before the first term of copyright expires, copyright protection is lost permanently and the work enters the public domain. The Copyright Office has no discretion to extend the renewal time limits.

(b) Renewal claims may be registered only in the names of persons falling within one of the classes of renewal claimants specified in the copyright law. If the work was a new version of a previous work, renewal may be claimed only in the new matter.

§ 202.18. **Notices of Use.**—Notices of use of copyrighted musical compositions on mechanical instruments, required by section 1(e) of title 17, U. S. Code, will be recorded upon receipt of a properly executed Form U and upon payment of the prescribed fees. Notices of intention to use will be received pursuant to section 101(e) of title 17, U.S. Code; no special form is provided therefor.

[SEAL]   ARTHUR FISHER,
Approved,   *Register of Copyrights.*
    L. QUINCY MUMFORD,
       Librarian of Congress.

Appendix C

Copyright Registration Form A

FORM A

CLASS	REGISTRATION NO.
A	DO NOT WRITE HERE

𝔄pplication for 𝔕egistration of a 𝔔laim to 𝔔opyright
in a published book manufactured in the United States of America

Instructions: Make sure that all applicable spaces have been completed before you submit the form. The application must be signed at line 10 and the *affidavit* (line 11) completed and notarized. The application should not be submitted until after the date of publication given in line 4, and should state the facts which existed on that date. For further information, see page 4.

Pages 1 and 2 should be typewritten or printed with pen and ink. Pages 3 and 4 should contain exactly the same information as pages 1 and 2, but may be carbon copies. Mail all pages of the application to the Register of Copyrights, Library of Congress, Washington 25, D. C., together with 2 copies of the best edition of the work and the registration fee of $4. Make your remittance payable to the Register of Copyrights.

1. Copyright Claimant(s) and Address(es): Give the name(s) and address(es) of the copyright owner(s). Ordinarily the name(s) should be the same as in the notice of copyright on the copies deposited.

Name _____

Address _____

Name _____

Address _____

2. Title: _____
(Give the title of the book as it appears on the title page)

3. Authors: Citizenship and domicile information must be given. Where a work was made for hire, the employer is the author. The citizenship of organizations formed under U. S. Federal or State law should be stated as U. S. A. Authors may be editors, compilers, translators, illustrators, etc., as well as authors of original text. If the copyright claim is based on new matter (see line 5) give requested information about the author of the new matter.

Name _____ Citizenship _____
(Give legal name followed by pseudonym if latter appears on the copies)   (Name of country)

Domiciled in U. S. A. Yes _____ No _____ Address _____

Name _____ Citizenship _____
(Give legal name followed by pseudonym if latter appears on the copies)   (Name of country)

Domiciled in U. S. A. Yes _____ No _____ Address _____

Name _____ Citizenship _____
(Give legal name followed by pseudonym if latter appears on the copies)   (Name of country)

Domiciled in U. S. A. Yes _____ No _____ Address _____

4. Date of Publication of This Edition: Give the date when copies of this edition were first placed on sale, sold, or publicly distributed. (NOTE: The full date (month, day, and year) must be given.)

5. New Matter in This Version: (NOTE: Leave this line blank unless the following instructions apply to this work.) If any substantial part of this work has been previously published, give a brief general statement of the nature of the new matter in this version. New matter may consist of compilation, translation, abridgment, editorial revision, and the like, as well as additional text or pictorial matter.

6. U. S. Edition of Book in English First Manufactured and Published Abroad: (NOTE: Leave this line blank unless the following instructions apply to this work.) If this is the U. S. edition of a book in English, and all or a substantial part of the English text of an earlier foreign edition was manufactured and first published abroad, complete the following spaces. *For further information, see page 4.*

Year date of first publication of foreign edition _____
(Year)

Was claim to ad interim copyright registered in the foreign edition?

| | Yes ☐ | No ☐ |

If claim to ad interim copyright was *not* registered, is U. S. copyright in the foreign edition claimed by virtue of the Universal Copyright Convention?

| | Yes ☐ | No ☐ |

Complete all applicable spaces on next page

7. If registration fee is to be charged to a deposit account established in the Copyright Office, give name of account:

8. Name and address of person or organization to whom correspondence or refund, if any, should be sent:

Name _____ Address _____

9. Send certificate to:

(Type or
print   Name _____
name and
address)   Address _____
                                        (Number and street)

                              _____
                              (City)   (Zone)   (State)

10. Certification: (NOTE: Application not acceptable unless signed)

I CERTIFY that the statements made by me in this application are correct to the best of my knowledge.

_____
(Signature of copyright claimant or duly authorized agent)

11. Affidavit (required by law). Instructions: (1) Fill in the blank spaces with special attention to those marked "(X)." (2) Sign the affidavit before an officer authorized to administer oaths within the United States, such as a notary public. (3) Have the officer sign and seal the affidavit and fill in the date of execution.

NOTE: The affidavit must be signed and notarized only *on or after* the date of publication or completion of printing which it states. The affidavit must be signed by an individual.

I, the undersigned, depose and say that I am the

STATE OF ....

COUNTY OF .... } *ss:*

☐ Person claiming copyright in the *book described in this application;

☐ The duly authorized agent of the person or organization claiming copyright in the book described in this application;

☐ The printer of the book described in this application.

That the book was published or the printing was completed on: (X) _____
                                                                (Give, month, day, and year)

That of the various processes employed in the production of the copies deposited, the setting of the type and the making of plates, or the lithographic or photoengraving processes used in producing the text, were performed within the limits of the United States, and that the printing of the text and the binding (if any) were also performed within the limits of the United States. That these processes were performed by the following establishments or individuals at the following addresses:
(GIVE THE NAMES AND ADDRESSES OF THE PERSONS OR ORGANIZATIONS WHO PRODUCED THE COPIES—TYPESETTERS, PRINTERS, BINDERS, ETC.)

Names (X) _____   Addresses (X) _____

_____   _____

_____   _____

_____
(Signature of affiant)
(Sign and notarize only on or after date given above)

PLACE
NOTARIAL SEAL   Subscribed and sworn to / affirmed before me this _____
HERE

day of _____, 19_____

_____
(Signature of notary)

FOR COPYRIGHT OFFICE USE ONLY	
Application and affidavit received	
Two copies received	
Fee received	
Renewal	

Certificate
Registration of a Claim to Copyright
in a published book manufactured in the United States of America

FORM A

CLASS	REGISTRATION NO.
A	DO NOT WRITE HERE

This Is To Certify that the statements set forth on this page have been made a part of the records of the Copyright Office. In witness whereof the seal of the Copyright Office is hereto affixed.

Register of Copyrights
United States of America

1. Copyright Claimant(s) and Address(es):

Name --

Address --

Name --

Address --

2. Title: --
(Title of book)

----

3. Authors:

Name --- Citizenship ------------------
(Legal name followed by pseudonym if latter appears on copies) (Name of country)

Domiciled in U. S. A. Yes -------- No -------- Address ------------------------------------

Name --- Citizenship ------------------
(Legal name followed by pseudonym if latter appears on copies) (Name of country)

Domiciled in U. S. A. Yes -------- No -------- Address ------------------------------------

Name --- Citizenship ------------------
(Legal name followed by pseudonym if latter appears on copies) (Name of country)

Domiciled in U. S. A. Yes -------- No -------- Address ------------------------------------

4. Date of Publication of This Edition:

----

5. New Matter in This Version:

----

6. U. S. Edition of Book in English First Manufactured and Published Abroad: If this is the U. S. edition of a book in English, and all or a substantial part of the English text of an earlier foreign edition was manufactured and first published abroad, complete the following spaces.

Year date of first publication of foreign edition ....
(Year)

Was claim to ad interim copyright registered in the foreign edition? Yes ☐ No ☐

If claim to ad interim copyright was *not* registered, is U. S. copyright in the foreign edition claimed by virtue of the Universal Copyright Convention? Yes ☐ No ☐

Complete all applicable spaces on next page

148

7. Deposit account: _____

8. Send correspondence to:

Name _____ Address _____

9. Send certificate to:

(Type or
print
name and
address)

Name _____

Address _____
(Number and street)

_____
(City) (Zone) (State)

Information concerning copyright in books

When To Use Form A. Form A is appropriate for published books which have been manufactured in the United States.

What Is a "Book"? The term "books" covers not only material published in book form, but also pamphlets, leaflets, cards, and single pages containing text. Books include fiction, nonfiction, poetry, collections, directories, catalogs, and information in tabular form.

Unpublished Books. The law does not provide for registration of "book" material in unpublished form. Unpublished books are protected at common law against unauthorized use prior to publication.

Duration of Copyright. Statutory copyright in published books lasts for 28 years from the date of first publication, and may be renewed for a second 28-year term.

How to secure statutory copyright in a book

First: Produce Copies With Copyright Notice. Produce the work in copies by printing or other means of reproduction. To secure copyright, it is essential that the copies bear a copyright notice in the required form and position, as explained below.

Second: Publish the Work With Copyright Notice. The copyright law defines the "date of publication" as ". . . the earliest date when copies of the first authorized edition were placed on sale, sold, or publicly distributed by the proprietor of the copyright or under his authority."

Third: Register Your Copyright Claim. Promptly after publication, mail to the Register of Copyrights, Library of Con-

gress, Washington 25, D. C., two copies of the work as published with notice, an application on Form A, properly completed and notarized, and a fee of $4.

The Copyright Notice. The copyright notice for books shall appear on the title page or verso thereof, and shall consist of three elements: the word "Copyright," or the abbreviation "Copr.," or the symbol ©, accompanied by the name of the copyright owner and the year date of publication. Example: © John Doe 1961. Use of the symbol © may result in securing copyright in countries which are members of the Universal Copyright Convention.

> NOTE: It is the act of publication with notice that actually secures copyright protection. If copies are published without the required notice, the right to secure copyright is lost, and cannot be restored.

Books manufactured abroad

In General. Form A is not appropriate for books which have been manufactured outside the United States.

Foreign-Language Books. Applications covering foreign-language books by foreign authors, manufactured abroad, should be submitted on Form A–B Foreign.

English-Language Books. Books in English manufactured abroad may be registered for "ad interim" copyright (Form A–B Ad Interim); or, if they are protected under the Universal Copyright Convention they are eligible for full-term registration on Form A–B Foreign:

(1) *Ad Interim Copyright.* Ad interim registration is necessary for protection in the United States unless copyright has

been secured under the Universal Copyright Convention. To secure ad interim copyright a claim must be registered within six months of first publication abroad. Ad interim copyright lasts for 5 years or until an American edition is published within the 5-year period and registered.

(2) *Universal Copyright Convention.* An English language work by a foreign author first published abroad is eligible for full-term U. S. copyright if: (a) its author is a citizen or subject of a country which is a member of the Universal Copyright Convention, or the work was first published in such country, and (b) all published copies bear the copyright notice provided under the Universal Copyright Convention.

FOR COPYRIGHT OFFICE USE ONLY		
Application and affidavit received		
Two copies received		
Fee received		

Appendix D

Universal Copyright Convention

List of Accessions

Andorra
Argentina
Austria
Belgium
Brazil
Cambodia
Canada
Chile
Costa Rica
Cuba
Czechoslovakia
Denmark
Ecuador
Finland
France
German Federal Republic

Ghana
Greece
Haiti
Holy See
Iceland
India
Ireland
Israel
Italy
Japan
Laos
Lebanon
Liberia
Liechtenstein
Luxembourg
Mexico

Monaco
Nicaragua
Nigeria
Norway
Pakistan
Panama
Paraguay
Peru
*Philippines
Portugal
Spain
Sweden
Switzerland
United Kingdom
United States of America

---

* UNESCO has advised the U.S. Government that on November 14, 1955, a letter was received from the Philippine Minister in Paris stating that the Philippine President had directed the withdrawal of the instrument of accession prior to November 19, 1955, the date on which the Convention would become effective in respect of the Philippines. No determination has been made as to the legal effect of this communication.

Appendix E

Signatories to Association
of American University Presses
Resolution on Permissions

The University of Arizona Press
Bollingen Foundation
The Brookings Institution
University of California Press
The University of Chicago Press
Columbia University Press
Cornell University Press
Duke University Press
Duquesne University Press
Fordham University Press
The University of Georgia Press
University of Hawaii Press
Huntington Library Publications
The University of Illinois Press
Indiana University Press
The Iowa State University Press
The Johns Hopkins Press
The University of Kansas Press
University of Kentucky Press
Louisiana State University Press
Loyola University Press

The M.I.T. Press
The Metropolitan Museum of Art
The Michigan State University Press
University of Missouri Press
University of Nebraska Press
The University of New Mexico Press
New York University Press
University of North Carolina Press
Northwestern University Press
University of Notre Dame Press
Ohio State University Press
Pennsylvania State University Press
The University of Pittsburgh Press
Princeton University Press
Smithsonian Institution
University of South Carolina Press
Southern Illinois University Press
Southern Methodist University Press

Stanford University Press
Syracuse University Press
University of Texas Press
University of Toronto Press

University of Washington Press
Wayne State University Press
The University of Wisconsin Press
Yale University Press

Appendix F

Book publication contract

1. The AUTHOR agrees to write for publication a work entitled
_____ . The AU-
THOR grants to the PUBLISHER the exclusive right to publish and sell the
work, under its own name and under other imprints or trade names,
during the full term of copyright and all renewals thereof, and to copyright it in the PUBLISHER's name or any other name in all countries, with
exclusive authority to dispose of said rights in all countries and in all
languages.

2. The manuscript, containing about _____ words, will be delivered to the PUBLISHER by the AUTHOR by _____ 19__.

3. The AUTHOR agrees to deliver the manuscript to the PUBLISHER
in typewritten form, in duplicate, with a third copy to be retained by
the AUTHOR. It will be in proper form for use as copy by the printer.
The content of the manuscript will be such as both the AUTHOR and
the PUBLISHER are willing to have appear in print.

4. The AUTHOR agrees to furnish the following items along with the
manuscript: title page; preface or foreword (if any); table of contents;
index; teacher's manual or key (if requested by the PUBLISHER); and
complete and final copy for all illustrations, properly prepared for reproduction.

5. The manuscript will be published at the PUBLISHER's own expense.
The PUBLISHER will pay the AUTHOR the following royalty, based on
either (1) the list price of the book, or (2) the actual cash received
from sales of the book by the PUBLISHER: _____

_____ .

6. The PUBLISHER will report to the AUTHOR on the sale of the work
twice each year for the six-month periods ending the prior December 31

and June 30, respectively. With each report of sales, the PUBLISHER will make settlement for any balance shown to be due.

7. The AUTHOR will read the proofs, correct them in duplicate, and promptly return one set to the PUBLISHER. The AUTHOR will be responsible for the completeness and accuracy of such corrections and will bear all costs of alterations in the proofs (other than those resulting from printer's errors) which exceed 10 per cent of the cost of typesetting. These costs will be deducted from the first royalty payments due the AUTHOR.

8. The PUBLISHER has the right to edit the work for the original printing and for any reprinting, provided that the meaning of the text is not materially altered.

9. The PUBLISHER has the right: (1) to publish the work in suitable style as to paper, printing, and binding; (2) to fix or alter the title and price; (3) to use all customary means to market the work.

10. The AUTHOR warrants that he is the sole owner of the work and has full power and authority to copyright it and to make this agreement; that the work does not infringe any copyright, violate any property rights, or contain any scandalous, libelous, or unlawful matter. The AUTHOR will defend, indemnify, and hold harmless the PUBLISHER against all claims, suits, costs, damages, and expenses that the PUBLISHER may sustain by reason of any scandalous, libelous, or unlawful matter contained or alleged to be contained in the work, or any infringement or violation by the work of any copyright or property right. Until such claim or suit has been settled or withdrawn, the PUBLISHER may withhold any sums due the AUTHOR under this agreement.

11. The AUTHOR warrants that the work contains no material from other copyrighted works without the other publisher's consent and the written consent of the owner of such copyrighted material. The AUTHOR will obtain such consents and file them with the PUBLISHER.

12. The AUTHOR agrees that during the term of this agreement he will not publish or furnish to any other publisher any work on the same subject that will conflict with the sale of this work.

13. The AUTHOR agrees to revise the work if requested to do so by the PUBLISHER. The provisions of this agreement apply to each revision of the work by the AUTHOR as though that revision were the work being published for the first time under this agreement. Should the AUTHOR not provide a revision within a reasonable time after the PUBLISHER has requested it, or should the AUTHOR be deceased, the PUBLISHER may have the revision prepared and charge the cost against the AUTHOR's royalties, and may display in the revised work, and in advertising, the name of the person or persons who revise the work.

14. The PUBLISHER may permit others to publish, broadcast by radio, make recordings or mechanical renditions, publish book-club and microfilm editions, make translations and other versions, show by motion pictures or by television, syndicate, quote, and otherwise utilize this

work and material based on this work. The net amount of any compensation received from such use shall be divided equally between the PUBLISHER and the AUTHOR. The PUBLISHER may authorize such use by others without compensation, if, in the PUBLISHER's judgment, such use may benefit the sale of the work. If the PUBLISHER itself uses the work for any of the foregoing purposes (other than publishing), the AUTHOR will be paid _____ per cent of the cash received from such use. On copies of the work or sheets sold outside the continental United States or sold by radio, television, mail-order, or coupon advertising direct to the consumer, the AUTHOR will be paid a royalty of _____ per cent of the cash received from such sales. If the PUBLISHER sells any overstock of the work at a price below the manufacturing costs of the book plus royalties, no royalties shall be paid. All copies of the work sold and all compensation from sales of the work under this paragraph shall be excluded in computing the royalties payable under paragraph 5 above and shall be computed and shown separately in reports to the AUTHOR.

15. If the balance due the AUTHOR for any settlement period is less than fifty dollars, the PUBLISHER will make no accounting or payment until the settlement period at the end of which the cumulative balance has reached fifty dollars. When the PUBLISHER decides that the public demand for this work no longer warrants its continued manufacture, the PUBLISHER may discontinue manufacture and destroy any or all plates, books, and sheets without liability to the AUTHOR.

16. The PUBLISHER will give six copies of the book to the AUTHOR without charge. Additional copies for the AUTHOR's use shall be supplied at a _____ discount from the list price.

17. This agreement may not be changed unless the parties agree in writing.

18. This agreement shall be construed and interpreted according to the laws of the State of California and shall be binding upon the parties hereto, their heirs, successors, assigns, and personal representatives; and references to the AUTHOR and to the PUBLISHER shall include their heirs, successors, assigns, and personal representatives.

_____

PUBLISHER

_____

AUTHOR

_____
Date

Appendix G

Contract for a magazine article

1. We hand you herewith our check for $2,000.00 in payment for all rights of every kind in the material, including the right to copyright and the right to use the author's name, biography, and likeness to advertise issues of our publications carrying the material. The author shall, as directed by us and at our expense, execute and deliver to us such applications or other documents and take such other steps from time to time as we request for the purpose of securing any copyrights or renewals thereof, or protecting copyrights obtained by us. Unless otherwise expressly agreed in writing, our renewal of any copyright shall automatically extend, for the renewal period, any assignment of rights made by us pursuant hereto.

2. We agree, upon one complete publication of the materials in one of our publications, and on written request, to assign to the author, his heirs, representatives, or assigns, all rights under our copyright in the material except all magazine rights (including the right to authorize or issue reprints) for the United States of America, its territories and possessions, and Canada.

3. Under our reservation of magazine rights the author or his assignee may advertise dramatic or motion-picture productions of the material, or any reissue or remake thereof or sequels thereto, through the presentation of new story versions based on such dramatizations or motion pictures, either in circular matter, press books, press notices, trade journals, and magazines devoted principally to dramatic or motion-picture matter; provided that such new story versions do not appear as having been written by the author, and do not exceed fifteen hundred (1500) words in length when based on a short story appearing complete in one issue,

or five thousand (5000) words when based on (a) a serial appearing in two or more issues, (b) a novelette or condensed novel appearing complete in one issue, or (c) a series of not less than three connected short stories or articles from which a single drama or motion picture is made.

4. The author shall protect our copyright by appropriate copyright notice in connection with any further publication made by him or his assigns pursuant to the rights assignable hereunder.

5. When selling or transferring any rights assignable to the author hereunder, the author shall give the vendee or transferee written notice of all applicable restrictions so that there shall be no misunderstanding, infringement, or impairment of our copyright or rights retained hereunder.

6. Your acceptance of this check constitutes your acceptance of this agreement.

THE MAGAZINE PUBLISHER

Appendix H

Suggested readings

This is not a bibliography, but only a list of suggestions for further reading. An effort has been made to suggest books that will be meaningful to the person who lacks legal training.

Publishing

Grannis, Chandler B., *What Happens in Book Publishing*. New York: Columbia University Press, 1957. A general survey of all aspects of book publishing.
Literary Market Place. New York: R. R. Bowker Company (published annually). The business directory of American book publishing; contains information on university presses and commercial book publishers, agents, artists and art services, book associations, book reviewers, editorial services, newspapers and news services, radio and television, sales representatives, translators, writers' conferences, and so forth.
Rosenthal, Richard, ed., *Writer's Market*. Cincinnati: Writer's Digest (published annually). Lists 3,500 markets for free-lance writers, mostly magazines and journals; also contains information on book publishers, radio and television markets, newspapers, plays, and so forth.
The Writers' and Artists' Year Book. London: Adam and Charles Black

(published annually). A directory of markets in Great Britain, Ireland, Canada, Australia, and other countries for writers, artists, photographers, and composers.

Copyright

Latman, Alan, ed., *Howell's Copyright Law*. Washington, D.C.: BNA Incorporated, 1962. A good handbook intended primarily for lawyers.

Lindey, Alexander, *Plagiarism and Originality*. New York: Harper & Brothers, 1962. An entertainingly written history of plagiarism.

Nimmer, Melville B., *Nimmer on Copyright*. Albany, San Francisco, New York: Matthew Bender & Co., 1963. The most up-to-date and comprehensive work on the subject. It will be the standard work for years to come.

Putnam, George H., *Authors and Their Public in Ancient Times*. New York: G. P. Putnam's Sons, 1894.

Putnam, George H., *Books and Their Makers During the Middle Ages*. New York: G. P. Putnam's Sons, 1896-97; reprinted by Hillary House, 1962.

Ransom, Harry, *The First Copyright Statute*. Austin: University of Texas Press, 1956. A history of the first English copyright law.

Patents

Brink, Richard E., Donald C. Grippe, and Harold Hughesdon, *An Outline of The United States Patent Law*. New York: Interscience Publishers, Inc., 1959. Tells how to obtain a patent and how to enforce the rights granted under it.

Buckles, Robert A., *Ideas, Inventions, and Patents: How to Develop and Protect Them*. New York: John Wiley & Sons, Inc., 1957. Intended primarily for engineers and scientists engaged in research and development activities, this book discusses means for the effective protection and exploitation of ideas and inventions.

Palmer, Archie M., *University Patent Policies and Practices*. Washington, D.C.: National Academy of Sciences, National Research Council, 1952 and 1955. Analysis of patent practices at major colleges and universities in the United States.

Academic Freedom and Tenure

Byse, Clark and Louis Joughin, *Tenure in American Education: Plans, Practices, and the Law*. Ithaca: Cornell University Press, 1959. The best work on the subject.

Chafee, Zechariah, Jr., *Free Speech in the United States*. Cambridge, Mass.: Harvard University Press, 1941. A classic work by a great scholar and wise man.

Hofstadter, Richard and Walter B. Metzger, *The Development of Academic Freedom in the United States*. New York: Columbia University Press, 1955. This and the following volume are general studies of academic freedom prepared for the American Academic Freedom project at Columbia University.

MacIver, Robert M., *Academic Freedom in Our Time*. New York: Columbia University Press, 1955.

Stewart, George R. (and others), *The Year of the Oath*. Garden City, New York: Doubleday & Company, Inc., 1950. An account of the loyalty oath controversy at the University of California.

Legal Biography

Beveridge, Albert J., *The Life of John Marshall*. Boston: Houghton Mifflin Company, 1916-19. The definitive biography of a great Chief Justice of the United States Supreme Court.

Bowen, Catherine D., *Yankee from Olympus: Justice Holmes and His Family*. Boston: Little, Brown & Co., 1944. The famous son of a famous father.

Bowen, Elizabeth, *The Lion and the Throne*. Boston: Little, Brown & Co., 1957. The best-selling life of Sir Edward Coke (1552-1634).

Mason, Alpheus T., *Brandeis: A Free Man's Life*. New York: The Viking Press, Inc., 1946. A first-rate biography of a great lawyer and judge.

Seagle, William, *Men of Law from Hammurabi to Holmes*. New York: The Macmillan Company, 1947. Biographies of fourteen important figures in legal history.

Stone, Irving, *Clarence Darrow for the Defense*. Garden City, New York: Doubleday & Company, Inc., 1941. The life of the great advocate and his turbulent career.

Law, Lawyers, and Society

Allen, Carleton K., *Law in the Making*. Oxford, England: The Clarendon Press, 1964 (7th edition). A study of the origin and development of law by a sometime Professor of Jurisprudence at Oxford.

Berman, Harold J., *Talks on American Law*. New York: Vintage Books, 1961. A series of broadcasts to foreign audiences by members of the Harvard Law School faculty.

Black, Charles L., Jr., *The People and the Court*. New York: The Macmillan Company, 1960. A study of the Supreme Court and judicial review by a professor at the Yale Law School.

Bok, Curtis, *I Too, Nicodemus*. New York: Alfred A. Knopf, Inc., 1946. A book about a wise, human judge and the cases that come before him.

Borchard, Edwin M., *Convicting the Innocent*. New Haven, Conn.: Yale University Press, 1932. A thought-provoking collection of cases involving a miscarriage of justice.

Brierly, James L., *The Law Of Nations*, 5th Ed. Oxford, England: The Clarendon Press, 1955. An excellent short introduction to international law.

Cahn, Edmond, *The Sense of Injustice*. New York: New York University Press, 1949. A witty, stimulating discussion of justice.

Cohen, Morris R., *Law and the Social Order*. New York: Harcourt, Brace & Co., 1933. A collection of essays by a great American philosopher who thought deeply about law.

Cozzens, James Gould, *The Just and the Unjust*. New York: Harcourt, Brace & Co., 1942. This has been called the best novel for lawyers to read.

Frank, Jerome, *Courts on Trial*. Princeton, N. J.: Princeton University Press, 1949. A lively work by the late judge on the administration of justice.

Gray, John Chipman, *The Nature and Sources of the Law*, 2nd Ed. New York: The Macmillan Company, 1921. One of the standard works in the field.

Hall, Margaret E., *Selected Writings of Benjamin N. Cardozo*. New York: Fallon Publications, 1947. Contains his four great works and other essays.

Hart, H. L. A., *Law, Liberty, and Morality*. Stanford, Calif.: Stanford University Press, 1963. A stimulating and persuasive work by an Oxford professor on the use of criminal law to enforce morality.

Hoebel, E. Adamson, *The Law of Primitive Man*. Cambridge, Mass.: Harvard University Press, 1954. A good starting place to obtain an understanding of law and society.

Hurst, James W., *The Growth of American Law*. Boston: Little, Brown & Co., 1950. A study of the contributions made to the development of American law by legislatures, courts, and bar.

Lerner, Max, ed., *The Mind and Faith of Mr. Justice Holmes*. Boston: Little, Brown & Co., 1943. A collection of Holmes' writings, with an illuminating introduction and commentary by the editor.

Mayers, Lewis, *The American Legal System*. New York: Harper, 1955. A systematic account of American legal institutions.

Morris, Herbert, ed., *Freedom and Responsibility*. Stanford, Calif.: Stanford University Press, 1961. A splendid collection of readings drawn from law and philosophy dealing with the broad topic of responsibility; a thoughtful introduction by the editor begins each chapter.

Plucknett, Theodore F. T., *A Concise History of the Common Law*, 3rd Ed. London: Butterworth & Co., 1940. Has been called the best short history of the growth of the law in England.

Radin, Max, *The Law and You*. New York: New American Library, 1948. A popular treatment by a very learned teacher of law.

Index

DATE DUE